FROM SUNSET TO SUNRISE

DON'T GIVE UP

A Darlene Gonzales
LifeScript

A SiSability Imprint
Turning My Own Pages Legacy Publishing

From Sunset to Sunrise
NEVER GIVE UP

Scripture quotations are taken from the following versions:
New Kings James Version (NKJV)
Amplified Bible (AMP)
The Living Bible (TLB)
New International Version (NIV)
All rights reserved. Used by permission.

ISBN: 9781676929499
Copyright by Darlene Gonzales

Published in the United States
SiSability Imprints: Author Coaching by Dr. Verlean Hailey Gould of Turning My Own Pages Legacy Publishing, Texas
Editing: Renée Purdie, www.msrisingstar.com
Cover and Interior Graphics by the Author Academy
Layout: Katie Brady - www.katiebradydesign.com

Printed in the United States of America
2019 – 1st SiSability Imprint Edition

DEDICATION

I dedicate this book to my beloved children, grandchildren, my family and to all who are struggling in one capacity or another. God is real and as you read this book, I want you to know that without a shadow of a doubt God loves you. Confess, and turn from your sins. Nothing is too hard for God.

Prayer of Dedication To My Readers
THE GOOD SOIL
Mark 4:14-20 New International Version (NIV)

[14] The farmer sows the word. 15 Some people are like seed along the path, where the word is sown. As soon as they hear it, Satan comes and takes away the word that was sown in them. 16 Others, like seed sown on rocky places, hear the word and at once receive it with joy. 17 But since they have no root, they last only a short time. When trouble or persecution comes because of the word, they quickly fall away. 18 Still others, like seed sown among thorns, hear the word; 19 but the worries of this life, the deceitfulness of wealth and the desires for other things come in and choke the word, making it unfruitful. 20 Others, like seed sown on good soil, hear the word, accept it, and produce a crop—some thirty, some sixty, some a hundred times what was sown."

When I first came to Christ, the Word was given to me and it was supposed to take root, but at the first sign of trouble, the enemy stole that seed, and deterred my path away from Christ temporarily. Now when I went back to Church, my commitment was like the rocky places, until the peer pressure came to use drugs again. My faith was not strong enough to stand up against that pressure. I did show signs of growth until money and the world tried to choke the Word that had been planted. But now I hear the Word, I put it into practice and now it remains in good soil.

Heavenly Father, as I devote this book to you, we pray this book will lead others to Christ, as my life is your story. I pray that they will never ever **give up** no matter what life brings their way. I pray that you will strengthen them, guide them and keep them as you have done for me. Cover them and catch them when they stumble. I pray that you give them a double portion of what you've given me. Amen!

TABLE OF CONTENTS

FORWARD

Life is about growth from experience. Ministry is about God using our life experiences to help others to grow. Darlene has opened her heart to God and God has been using her and will continue to use her to reach out to others and share about His goodness. It's not about how life starts out for you. It's about what you end up doing in and with your life.

I have had the fortunate opportunity to be one of Darlene's mentors and it has been a blessing to witness her growth.

May the LORD bless all who read and hear her story. May the LORD continue to use her and may the territory of her ministry continue to expand.

Be Blessed!

The Reverend Miriam Bacon

INTRODUCTION

A life script describes the meaning we attribute to the events that happen to us. Depending on our particular script, we can interpret an event in various ways.

Social Scientists believe that our life scripts are usually created in childhood, long before our brains have matured, which for most of us is at 26. By then we have experienced enough trauma from our family dynamics and social constructs that we have predictable responses to life challenges. Understanding our particular LifeScript can help us see how it might influence our thoughts and may help us come up with more positive thoughts and actions. If our thoughts and actions are not subject to the wisdom of God for our lives, we may find that we are continuing addictive patterns that get us nowhere near our hopes and dreams. The Bible says, a righteous man will fall seven times but will rise again (Proverbs 24:16) NKJV. Life happens! You might say stuff happens, but when GOD takes control, when we yield to His leading and guiding, our LifeScripts change. In fact—we change; we recover; we grow—IF WE DON'T GIVE UP!!!

Your life script is individual to you, but many follow a common theme. To uncover your life script, it helps to explore the patterns in your life, particularly if you suspect that there are destructive themes in your script. In this book, Darlene Gonzales shares her destructive themes. Her LifeScript is powerfully sad, but because she refused to GIVE UP, we find her not only embracing a new life and a faithful God, we find her giving life to those who have experienced some of what she endured, and may have doubted that life would ever change for the better.

In From Sunset to Sunrise, journey with Darlene as she takes you to the depth of pain, sorrow, abandonment, addiction, and spiritual warfare into the place of faith that eventually makes her whole and HIS.

Verlean Hailey, Ph.D.
Turning My Own Pages Legacy Publishing
Writer's Coach

LifeScript 1

BIG DREAMS SOMETIMES DIE

As a little girl growing up on the south side in Phoenix, Arizona, I had what seemed to me to be big dreams: dreams of my mother living with us, dreams of having free time to play and to be a kid, dreams of my mom doing my hair and teaching me proper etiquette. As many young girls dreamed of being married, owning a nice home, and having a few children and taking family vacations in their station wagon, it never happened for me. However, although we didn't have much, I do remember being reasonably happy and content. We never brought used clothing. We shopped at Sears and Roebuck, Kmart and Globe. My father was a strong man. I wasn't raised by my mother, so I really don't have many memories growing up with her as my other siblings did, only later in my adult life. We lived close by an elementary school and my entire family attended at one time or another. I dreaded going to school; the kids were so mean, and I was usually picked on. When I got in trouble the Principal usually called my father and one time, and I mean one time only, he spanked me. I do not remember the reason why, but I was not the only kid standing in line for a paddling. When I got home, I told my father and he had a little talk with the Principal. From that point on whenever I got in trouble, he would call my father and I hated when my Father came to school. The kids would say whose father was that, etc. My father's skin was lighter, and his hair was curly. So, when he came on campus to an almost 98% African

American school, it surely seemed that he was out of place. I did not want anyone to know that he was my father. I know this is "a shame," but I was already getting picked on.

When I reached Junior High School, I learned my father could not read or write. I started noticing things that I am pretty sure my older siblings knew. When he would attempt to cash a check, he would mark an X for his signature. I remember one time, he asked me to teach him how to read. It did not last long, as other things got in the way of him studying. Mostly it was his pride.

We lived in a three-bedroom house with part of a carport my father turned into a den. This was something that my Father owned, and he was so proud of his home. At the end of the gates, two flag poles were attached, one on each side of the gate. One was an African-American flag and the other was a Cuban Flag. I thought we were rich. My Father was an entrepreneur. He took care of us by landscaping yards in the rich neighborhoods like "Scottsdale." There were five of us living in the home, all by the same mother, three boys and two girls. On Saturdays, I would stay home with my sister "olive oil" while my father and my brothers left for work very early in the morning. My sister and I, if I chose to get up, were to make their sandwiches for lunch. After they left, my sister usually got started early doing the laundry. We had a huge metal ringer washing machine with two metal tubs attached that rinsed the clothes as they passed through the ringer. We may have been the only family at that time that still had one. I remember Olive Oil getting her arm stuck in that thing one day. I thought I would pass out as she was screaming. My Father came out and turned it off and set her free by unplugging it and raising the rollers. I just knew she lost her arm, but she did not, but she still has the scar to this day. It sucked her arm in up to the fold in her elbow.

My Father had a lot of friends and would throw a party "at the drop of a hat." Olive Oiland I would oversee making the snacks and my Father would get his grill started by looking for the right wood. It would take him days to find the wood to cook with. He had the largest handmade grills I had ever seen. My Father was an amazing cook and when people found out how his food tasted, they started to ask him to make some for them and that's when it started. He made menudo, barbeque sauce and sometimes his famous potato salad. We would spend hours in that yellow kitchen cutting up ingredients. Word got around and he then began to sell his barbeque sauce and menudo in large pickle jars. No matter what we ate, we had jalapeños to eat with it. We had chickens for days: baked chicken, barbequed chicken, grilled chicken, chicken and dumplings, chicken and rice, chicken stew, etc.

When they'd return from working, my Father had a routine. He would have a can of Schlitz Malt Liquor and lay his clothes out. He would give us our allowances, take a bath, get dressed and go out clubbing. He was a good dancer and the ladies loved him. Or sometimes, he'd have his friends over and have big stake domino games. And I was the chip girl! I loved it. I got to see how they played, and I had a chance to spend more time with my Father.

In our backyard, we had a few animals: our dog named Big Foot, a horse named Smokey, some chickens and ducks. I remember my Father telling us girls that he did not want us messing with the horse. He also told my brothers repeatedly to not walk behind the horse. Well, one day my brother walked behind the horse, he was knocked out for hours. I always wondered why my Father never awakened him. He kept on doing what he was doing in the backyard, but he did stay close by him. I loved it when my Father would load us up in the back of the truck and take us to Thrifty's to get some ice cream. I'd always get butter pecan and to this very day that is my favorite flavor. My Father would also take us to a place near the airport where you can see the planes take off and land at night. We were not the only families there. We'd have our blankets and either lay on top of the truck or in the bed of the truck to see these powerful, huge machines land. It was the thing to do on a Sunday night. At times, my father would put us in the back of the truck, and he would load the dog in as well and we would go far out to a field, and he'd let Big Foot roam through the field. Nine out of ten times, he'd come running back with jack rabbits, and we knew that would be dinner. Well, I would not eat the jack rabbit. Sometimes I ate leftovers or nothing at all, but it was my choice. However, my Father knew so he would always have a side dish made.

There were other times when my Father would borrow our neighbor's boat and we would load up the cooler with bologna sandwiches, soda and his beer and we would drive to Roosevelt Lake. My Father had a camper that he would attach to the truck and we would ride back there. At times, I would sleep in there on the way. I remember the yellow shag carpeting that was in it. He loved fishing and outdoor activities.

I remember Olive Oil raising "Rhode Island Reds." She was so proud of her chickens. One day she wandered in the backyard just in time to see our Father wringing a chicken's neck. She freaked out! She did not know why he was killing the chickens, until he explained to her that we had to eat and that the yard chickens were better that the chickens in the store. He did promise not to kill the ones she raised, although eventually he did, when she left our home and moved in with her boyfriend. Eventually they got married … after my Father threatened him.

I grew up fast and being the only young lady of the house, I took over Olive Oil's role. We had a refrigerator that would leak water in the bottom of the vegetable tray, and it had to be cleaned every other day or it would spill out. I had to do the laundry, dusting and all the other housework. I remember starting my menstrual period. I was terrified to say the least. I have heard girls talk in the lady's bathroom in high school as they smoked their joints, but I did not know how they knew they had their periods. They were so proud of becoming a "Woman." One day, I started having some terrible stomach pains like never before. My Father was not at home. I remember my Mother calling and asking to speak to my Father. He wasn't there of course. So, I told her about my stomach pains, and she told me to take some of my Father's Excedrin, but she did not say anything else. Early that next morning, well you can guess what happened and since I had no one to show me anything I had to pad my underwear with toilet paper for that night. I attempted to use tampons like I heard the girls talking about at school in the ladies' room as we were ditching class and smoking weed. However, they caused me so much pain as I was not using them correctly. Eventually I learned! And yes, I smoked weed in the girl's bathroom when I did go in there and later began to sell pin heads (marijuana joints).

I admired my Father so much, especially after learning that he could not read nor write did not stop him from taking care of us kids, and the adult children that my Mother previously had. With that said, my Father had a temper, and we knew it. When we did something wrong, he would spank us with a belt. He had a nickname in the hood. It was "Killa." He did not blink twice in pulling out his gun. And the neighborhood knew it. You'd have to provoke him though. He did not just go around waving his gun. It took a lot of provoking to get him to this point.

I remember my Father going to the doctor because he was having some stomach problems. The doctor said it was because he was eating too many chili peppers. He had acid reflux and took medications for it as well as high blood pressure. But he continued the same eating lifestyle that he was raised with. He made vinegar and garlic water drinks and kept them in the refrigerator. He drank it faithfully every day for his high blood pressure. Boy did that stuff stink! Every so often he would gather us kids up to take our medicine: castor oil, Black-Draught or suppositories. I do not remember us kids getting sick with the flu or anything. We were always getting cleaned out.

My oldest brother soon left home, so it was only me and my little brother left. I was in High School. My Father tried not to take me out of school so much, but he did not have the help that he used to as my older brother was gone, my youngest was drunk half the time and my father could not go and do it alone. Helping my Father took so much time from my schooling that I eventually dropped out to help pay the bills and then my Father's stomach issues got worse. My Father used to tell me all the time, "Get your education. They may take away your freedom, but they can never take away what you know," as he pointed to his head.

I began working at my first job, Carl's Jr. I was the best at working the drive through window. I never had a car pulled to the front because of a system I created. I loved getting a paycheck. It helped us out a lot. It was all great until one day a young man had the nerve to call me a nigger. Why did he do that? My father walked into Carl's Jr's and saw that I was crying and asked me what was wrong. I didn't want to tell him because I loved my job. I told him and he threatened to kill the manager and the young man, who by the way was in the corner crying very loudly after my father got through threatening him. I lost my job. I was sad; I loved making my own money.

Soon afterwards my younger brother left home and it was just us two. I cooked, most of the time now, cleaned and worked. I wanted to go back to school but I couldn't. I was behind and everyone that I knew when I was there had graduated already. To me it would have been embarrassing to go back. Besides, I could not do that to my father. He needed me and I could not leave him as my other siblings had. He took out a mortgage on our home, which was paid for at that time.

We as kids were sheltered from the world. I guess that's why my older siblings left home. I was not allowed to go to dances, dates, etc. I knew nothing about life outside my Father's house. I found out years later that I was given the nickname "Church Girl" in high school. It was because I went nowhere, and I did not dress showing half my body as the other young ladies did. I had no freedom and thought my Father was keeping something from me when he was protecting me as a Father should. He was a Father to me and not a dad. To me. Fathers sacrifice; dads donate! He sacrificed for all of us, even the children my Mother had by other men. He will always be my hero.

I was about sixteen and a half when I lost my virginity. I met this young man in Maryvale, a type of suburban area for blacks in the Phoenix metro area. He was a friend of my cousin whose home we visited quite often, especially during football season. My father was a Dallas Cowboys fan and my cousin was a Pittsburgh Steelers fan. My boyfriend would sneak his Mom's car and drive to see me on the southside. We would make out on the side of the house. I was so scared that my father would drive up, as he tended to turn off his engine and coast up to the house. One day we were cutting it too close and I heard my father cut off his engine. I told him to run; I just knew we were both dead. My father saw the car pull off, but did not know if it was coming from the neighbor's house or not. Oh my goodness, that was close! I eventually took the bus one day to his house while his mother was at work and we had sex. I just knew my father could tell, as I thought I was walking funny. I guess all young ladies who lose their virginity feel that way the day after. He then began to get in trouble and his mother sent him back home to stay in Kansas City

My father's stomach issues got worse, and he was taken to an assisted living facility where they attempted to give him liquid shakes. He did not like it at all.

At the age of sixteen and a half, I was sent to my mother to live. At the age of seventeen and a half, I had my first child. She was a hard birth. I was in labor for three days. Nothing worked to ease that pain. Eventually they put me in the hospital and the father of my child walked with me through the hospital. I remember saying to myself, "I am not ready for this." I had no one to teach me anything. But who does? It was an experience I'll never forget. No one told me three days had passed while I was in labor and delivery. When it was time to deliver, the father of my child went in with me. I pushed, cursed, and screamed and he held my hand. After she was born, the doctor asked the father if he wanted to cut the umbilical cord. Guess who almost lost consciousness. He almost dragged me off the table. After it was cut and they tended to him, he walked off with her to show the family—who, by the way, had cooked every day while I was there. They brought food in: enchiladas, tacos etc.

Back to my father … he was very well known with the nurses and doctors as he cursed his way through each staff member who attempted to not allow him to eat regular food. Months later I took my daughter to see him. He said, "She looks just like him" and he loved her long hair. We spent hours at the visit. I didn't know that would be the last time I got to speak to my Father, or the last time he would come home. In fact, he never left the hospital.

What started out as heartburn turned into acid reflux, which turned into tumors and eventually stomach cancer. My sister being the oldest had to make the choice to do surgery to try and remove most of the cancer. They gave him a 50/50 chance of survival. I could not have made that choice, but she did. After his surgery, he was in ICU. He was not able to hear us, but his eyes were open. My sister and family begged me to go and see him, but it took me a while to go. I just did not want to see him in that way, not my strong courageous hero! I was told he did not have long, so I went trudging the halls of the hospital. Getting into the ICU was like getting into a well locked down unit in jail or prison. As I walked to the desk, speaking through the window asking for my Father, the nurse led me in and showed me where the bed was. As I walked up to the bed, a nurse had just finished changing his bandage which was huge. As I grabbed his hands, he squeezed it. She said, "he can't hear you," so I am not sure why I said, "Daddy, it's me." Just then his eyes opened, and I saw a tear stream down his cheeks. I begged him not to leave me, as more tears streamed down the side of his face as well as mine. This was the first time in my life I cried from my gut. It actually felt like something had punched me in my gut. It also felt as if the world around me went silent. He must have felt me trembling as he squeezed my hand. I do not remember how long I stayed; however, a few days after I left, he passed.

When my father took his last breath, so did I. The next twenty-three years of my life were spent trying to "breathe." After his passing, I had a longing for a father figure, someone who would step in and guide, protect and care for me. Before I knew God, I expressed my longing for him in hurtful ways. I was so vulnerable to the evil that was around me in the world that I became a part of it. I was so much a part of it that doing wrong and anger became second nature to me.

My world literally crashed. My life felt as if it sunk away with him. My Father, my protector, my hero, my provider was gone. *What will I do? Who will provide for me? Where will I go? Who will love me like he did?* I knew of no one, but him. After his funeral I found out that he left me money through his life insurance, which was used to pay for the remainder of his burial. The sheltered life as I knew it was over. After his passing, I began using another drug called crack cocaine.

Living with my mother and the rest of my siblings took some getting used to. I was not used to living with so many people; I was not used to having a lot of food only once a month when food stamps arrived and/or the checks on the first or third of the month. It took some getting used to. My sister Mary could make a pot of soup out of whatever was left in the refrigerator. She was an amazing cook. I remember the first time I tasted government cheese, peanut butter and canned meat. She made delicious cookies out of the peanut butter; delicious burritos from the canned meat and grilled cheese sandwiches that would make you think they came from a restaurant.

When I had my first child, I realized the advantages that I had on those government funded programs called Section 8, food stamps and welfare Checks. As I look back, I see how that type of government assistance helped keep me down and not wanting to do anything with my life. It was only supposed to be temporary, but temporary can turn permanent if you're not careful.

I remember I used to attempt to sneak down to Buckeye Road, where the pool halls and juke joints were, a mile and a half long of drugs, bars, gambling and prostitutes. My oldest brother saw me one time and ran me home. He told me if he ever saw me down there again, he would kick my

&*^. The next weekend I made it halfway down the block without seeing my brother. One of his friends told him where I was. He came in and threatened the man that I was talking to and put me in the car and threatened me too. I was so scared. Later that year he married and moved to California. He moved around a lot. My oldest brother Floyd was a mastermind at hustling. I remember a story of him getting an old floor-model television back in the day, filling it with rocks and selling it downtown near the courthouse. I learned a lot and saw a lot living with my mother. It was there I realized that I had been sheltered.

When I moved out on my own, I had a lot of help with babysitting and learning to be a mother. My mother was a huge help as well as my oldest sister Mary. She never had children of her own, so all of our children became hers. We had a lot of picnics and family gatherings. I began to drink, smoke weed as well as tried my first line of cocaine. I really did not notice anything from snorting a line of cocaine, so I tried smoking it, and that became my vice and eventually my downfall.

Growing up I fell in love with the movie "The Wizard of Oz." I loved Dorothy's determination, zeal, focus and boldness never to give up on her dream of going back home. Somewhere over her rainbow, her skies were blue and the dream she dared to dream did come true. Well, the dreams I spoke of in the beginning: dreams of marriage, a station wagon etc. took a wrong turn somewhere. Instead I went down the road of the love of money, which led to living "la vida loca", drugs and a broken heart. Inevitably that ride I was on, that ride of living the fast life, living against the law, thinking it was me against the world, never took me anywhere I wanted to go.

LifeScript 2

GUILTY AS CHARGED

After surviving two baby daddies, being pregnant five times with two stillborn, I realized that life as I knew it was going to get harder. I was in and out of jail in Phoenix. All my charges from 1992 to 1996 were for domestic violence, assault, assault with a deadly weapon and theft. I am not proud of these charges; however; I have them and have learned from them. For the first charge, assault with a deadly weapon, the weapon was an Easter egg. It happened in early 1992. My oldest sister Mary (RIP) and I argued a lot. The argument that day was over whether she wanted my children to go to the Easter egg hunt. Well, as I told her they were not her kids, and she did not buy any of the food. Therefore, they were going. She was doing my daughter's hair at the time of the argument. Just then she pulled her ponytail and my daughter began to cry. So, we begin arguing and it became very heated quickly. The police showed up and I would not shut up. So, my sister played the victim, lying about the events that took place. I felt like the officer that was taking my statement was not taking my side so to shut my sister up, I threw an Easter egg at her and off to jail I went. The jail in downtown Phoenix's booking area had a nickname, "The Horseshoe," because of its shape. This was the first in a line of long charges that would follow. It was scary; I was put in with prostitutes, gang members, women pimps, alcoholics, drug addicts and the homeless. You name it, it was in there.

The first jail cell was packed. It's the jail cell that you go in after being fingerprinted. At least sixty women were packed in like sardines, with only two metal bunk beds, a toilet with no toilet paper and a wall that hid only the bottom part of your body. Everyone had their eye on the bunk beds. If your name was called, you were moved one cell over, closer to the end of the horseshoe where the Judge was. When I stepped in, well I was pushed in by the guards, the women were asked to move back. Women were on the floor sleeping. I smelled feet and urine. I was shocked but I had to keep a straight face, or I would be punked and who knows what else. That was not happening on my watch. There were more African Americans in there than any other culture so when a Caucasian woman came in for drunk driving and she had some really nice shoes on, it became really interesting.

One of the women had brought a crack pipe in and was offering crack hits to anyone with a lighter. I guess as a frequent flier you began to "know the law" and expect to be released. She began to pick on this Caucasian woman, complimenting her hair and shoes. As I lay on the floor, I peeped up and noticed that she had no shoes on. She responded by thanking her for the compliments. Just then the black woman said, "What size are your shoes?" I got up as I could see where the conversation was going. She answered and the black woman said, "Those look like my shoes I left when they were patting me down." The other lady replied, "No these are mine." The black woman then said, "No, those are mine and I need you to take them off."

At that time, a couple of the really tough looking prostitutes told her to leave it alone and that she could get some shoes that were left by other women when she gets out. They did not want any trouble with the guards and said there were too many of us in there for them to shoot tear gas at one bad mouthed crackhead. Well, she did not listen, so she gave her two minutes to take her shoes off and give them to her. She didn't, and at that time, the guards noticed that we all were standing around the two women on the floor and began to ask what was going on. No one said anything.

Just then the black woman said, "Time's up," and she began to take the lady's shoes off. The Caucasian Woman hit her so hard, she knocked her out! Then she stood up and said, "Ain't nobody taking my shoes." The prostitutes told her to "sit her white &^% down and shut the *^% up. We ain't no crackheads' we will beat the white *^& out of you. The only reason we did not jump in is because she had that coming to her." Just then the guards came and asked what was wrong with her. Someone said, "She finally went to sleep," and we all began to laugh. I was then moved to the next cell, then the next, until I was released. Upon release, I had promised to attend anger management classes and bring back the signed sheet of attendance to the Judge within six weeks. Well, I went back in six weeks, but I did not have a signed paper of attendance. I told the Judge I was getting angry sitting in there and I did not want to go back. The Judge told me that was too bad because I had to go back or do ten days in jail. I told him I would try. Well, I did try, but I just could not keep my mouth shut. My opinion did not matter, only what the Facilitator said. No one told me that! I was asked to leave after the second day. The next week, I went back to apologize and asked for another chance. He gave it to me and said that he had to write the Judge about the two days I was suspended. Cool, I thought as long as I am back. After six weeks, I was done. Did I learn anything? No! Did I attend with the attempts of learning anything? No! After my Father's passing, I became bitter and angry and it showed. I showed up in court and the Judge dismissed the charge, but I had to pay for the two days that I was kicked out. I chalked it up to a learned lesson and got a job doing day labor, cleaning offices at the airport and paid the fine.

Later, I was arrested again for arguing with my brother. The only reason why I went to jail was my Mom's lamp was broken as I had knocked it over as I pulled a knife on my brother. I was booked on destruction of property and released the next day, as my Mom told my brother not to press charges against me since he started it. I had bought my mom a new lamp. As I look back now, I realize that my drinking and drug use were becoming more and more the fuel of my anger.

Early in 1993, I began slanging dope, cooking dope and smoking dope. All the while, my Mother looked after my children. I don't know what I would have done without her. As I look back, I feel that I took advantage of her kindness. At times I'd be gone days and weeks at a time. I'd call to check in, but it was not like me being there. As I began to venture out, I learned the rules of the streets. I learned that you must familiarize yourself with the people who were out there. You did not step on anyone's territory, but all customers were up for grabs. You learned to hide your stash 100 feet or more away from you so as not to get caught or you can use the "cabbage patch it" method. It kept us safe.

There were crackheads that would attempt to rob us at times, so I purchased a pink, pearl-handled, silver-plated 22. We had to always be on the lookout. There was a saying on the streets, "Never get high off your own supply." I could never make it big time because I was doing just that. I was selling enough to get by on and to re-up. When I had pinched down my product, sold small dimes and huge twenties, I had it made when there were crumbs in the bag. I would also make primos, marijuana or cigarettes laced with crack cocaine, to keep from smoking all my dope. I never prostituted my body, but I was always entertained by men who loved to wine and dine a beautiful black woman. It had gotten so hot on the block that SWAT began patrolling in the hood where we were serving particular anthe apartment complex. The ones who were not doing drugs began to move out or so we thought. Only a couple of people moved out in the back of the complex.

One night as I was hanging out on the block, my eye captured this fine light-skinned man. He was not tall in stature, but he had a reputation. He showed up every day on the block at a certain time of the day. I began to come out in the evening time as he did to get a chance to meet him. I heard a lot about him and I began to have a crush on him. I soon realized that coming out that late and staying up that late did not benefit me financially and I was not able to spend time with my kids, to do anything with them and my Mom was on my case. So, I went back to my regular hours, and soon I found out he was asking about me.

We met eventually and began to hang out. He was from Cali and that day that I first saw him was the day he came back. He frequented Cali a lot. Months would go by. We became an item. Bonnie and Clyde is what some called us. He found out that I was able to get my hands on crack cars and decided that he wanted to get in on it as well. I came to find out he was running stolen cars from Phoenix to a chop shop in California.

"Clyde" and I began to frequent this one apartment. The lady lived alone, and we knew her place would be a good place to hide out at. She was also a good informant ("snitch") for us. As we dragged ourselves into her house at 4:30 am, she told us something strange was going on with her neighbor. She saw them leaving and asked where they were going, they told her they were moving out. I asked, "What's so strange about that?" She said; the lights go off and on at strange times and you can smell food coming from the house and it's dark, but I can see a candle or a little light coming from there and not only that, one night I walked by and heard a radio. Yep, it was the Five–O! We decided to get a backup room at the Holiday Inn. A week had passed, and it became really eerie in the apartment complex. There was a U-Haul in the back of the complex and I noticed that it had been there for three days. Who in the hood can afford a U-Haul for that long and who in the hood had that much stuff to move? Besides it did not move. So, as I was talking with "Clyde," but as usual he did not listen. He would say, "Girl, you trippin'." So, when I bet him a hundred dollars that U-Haul has not moved and will not move and that it was full of a team of SWAT, the same SWAT team that was in that apartment. One night to prove me wrong, he crept up on the truck, and leaned back as if to tie his shoes. He proceeded to mark the back tire of the passenger side and the front passenger tire with a white bingo marker to see if it moved or not. Three days passed and sure enough it had not moved. He handed over the money and we stayed off the block until it was raided. They did not catch the people who we hung out with, as we hipped them to the sting. After it was raided, the tenants of the complex told us the "SWAT" team jumped out of the U-Haul.

Clyde was going to Cali again and he asked me if I wanted to go, so I went. It was thrilling. He dropped me off at a swap meet and picked me up as we took the Greyhound back to Phoenix. I went with him on a few of these trips. The last trip I took with him got tricky as the police were hot on our trail. He knew a lot about cars, especially cars from California as they had the low jack device. This one particular time, he pulled up on the block in a Mercedes Benz. He had taken the man's credit cards as well and left him in the hotel with lots of dope and a prostitute to keep him busy. He pulled up, asked me to get in and asked if I wanted to go to Cali that night? I said, "Yes." As we were headed out, we decided to pull into a park, use the restrooms and head out. Well, as I was in the lady's restroom, I heard police radios, I began to shake. They came in on me and asked me to come out with my hands up. As the ghetto bird's light illuminated the park, they were not able to find Clyde. I said to myself, "Where the *&^ did he go?" Another police car pulled up on the scene; this time it had K9 onboard. They found him. He had covered himself with sand in the sand box. I said to myself, "Why didn't I think of that?" They put us together and stood us both behind the police cars as they talked. He said to me I don't know you and you don't know me. I agreed, and I am glad that I did as they had been looking for him for a while and they were on his trail for a year or so.

I was arrested for vagrancy and guilt by association and sentenced to ten days in the Maricopa County Jail. I had to self-surrender, as I had never had a Failure to Appear "FTA" on my record. There who in their right mind would turn themselves in? Who would do this? This isn't right." Just then, the guard came out and asked if I was alright. I told him "Yes, I am trying to figure out the reasoning behind the mental torture of turning yourself in." After forty-five minutes, I rang the bell on the door, gave them my name and in I went.

I had remembered the talk on the street, and the news that they were going to build what they called "Tent City." I did not think anything of it, because I did not believe I'd ever go back to jail, and I did not believe that they would put women in tents. Well, I was mistaken. The time in the Horseshoe was scary, but compared to my first time being locked up, I was terrified. This one prison movie that I had seen on television played through my head. I remember this one show that we watched at my mother's called Cell Block-H. It was originally a British soap opera. It was a show of power, drugs and control. Some of the female inmates had the upper hand on the COs and vice versa. It was an interesting show on what seems to go on in a women's lock up.

I remember surrendering all my property. They took my clothes and all other items I had. I remember the lady correctional officer " Co"told me to go in this room. As I walked in naked, she followed behind me and asked me to squat and cough as she squatted in front of me to see if I had any contraband hidden in areas that were not to be seen by anyone else, especially a woman. I was humiliated, embarrassed, belittled and appalled that she could do this type of work. Not only that but she did not bat an eye. When that was over, I was given my outfit to put on, jail house slippers, toothpaste, a big towel and a small towel, a blanket and pillow. As I followed the guard down this long hallway, I heard women talking. Just then I was outside of my Pod and I was not alone as two other women were escorted by other guards. They had been transferred from another pod.

I was given my bunk, and one of the ladies on the bottom bunk helped me make my bed. She told me her name and shared that she keeps to herself and encouraged me to do the same. It was lunch time and she sat next to me. As we were eating, she told me to not ever take a small letter folded like a kite from anyone. She also told me if any of the women she pointed out were in the showers not to go in. They would either rape me or they would be in there doing drugs and I did not want to get caught in that. Basically, she said to, "Keep your eyes open and watch your back." After the first few days, I became somewhat at ease and began to play cards and dominos. As the evening of the third day seemed to be over, we were notified that we would be transferring to the tents. There was a lot of uproar, to the point we were put on lock down. I was angry about the lock down, as I wanted to watch television. I had two days and a wake up to go before I got out.

The next morning, we were given our new outfits of black and white stripes; I was not there long enough for the pink. I was shocked at what they had done. Not only that, I remember the guard escorting me and three more ladies to where we would be staying. I chose the top bunk knowing that there were critters out there. I was bunked "housed" under the huge watchtower with its huge red vacancy neon flashing lights. I was outdone at that time. I wanted to get out fast. The next day, the news cameras came, and I asked not to be photographed. I did not want anyone to see me in this place, especially my children. I was released and took the bus to my Mother's house.

It was not long after being at my mother's that I went back to what I knew, the street life. And it was not long after I got out that my Mother along with my sister kicked me and my children out of her house. I remember this well. I had just given her half of the rent and went grocery shopping and put close to over two hundred dollars of food in her refrigerator. I sat down to comb my daughter's hair when the phone rang, and my Mother walked outside. I did not think anything of it until fifteen minutes later or so a knock was on the door. I knew right away who it was. It was the Phoenix Police Department "PPD". The officer asked my name and told me that me and my children had ten minutes to gather all our things and leave the property. I began to argue with him while trembling inside. "Wait 'till my Mother gets back! This is a mistake!" He opened the door and pointed across that way and there stood my mother and my sister. I was floored to say the least. I could not believe it! I found out after my children and I went to the Holiday Inn that my sister, her husband and her children moved in with my Mother. You mean to tell me that you and your husband could not keep a roof over your heads, while you were working as a Correctional Officer and he was at a reputable utilities company? Something is wrong with that! Anyway, this was another instance God watched over me and my children.

I grabbed a backpack and put my children's things in them. When we walked out, my mother and sister were not there. I had nowhere to take my children. So, we sat at the bus stop on the corner of Camelback Road. After hours had passed, I noticed a van that drove by twice. Finally, he stopped and asked if everything was alright. I told him we had nowhere to go. He told us to get in and I did. I had my gun, so I was not worried about anything. He took us to the Holiday Inn on the strip that I used to where I used to see drugs at.. He had just gone grocery shopping and gave me and my children a loaf of bread, water and a cooler. He told me that it would be good if I had a microwave as well.

There I was with my children in a two-bed hotel on the Strip. We made it work for a while. My children would constantly ask for my mother. I would call her for them, and they would be on the phone for hours telling her what was going on. As I look back, my mother was probably tired of my mess, but you do not put your grandchildren out in the street. I can survive, but not them. There were plenty of times when I left them in the hotel alone to go to the Strip to sell dope in order to pay for the room for the next couple of days and if it was a good night I'd pay for a week.

As time went on, my mother convinced me to go back to her house. One day during the first of the month, as she always did, she went to the store to get laundry soap, quarters and a little grocery shopping. My job was to clean out the refrigerator and clean the house. It was taking her a long time to come back and we were worried. We soon received a call from Phoenix Police that she was in a bad car accident. My family rushed to the hospital to check on her. Me, I got high! I had just lost my father. I was not equipped for losing anyone else. One of my smoking buddies took me to the hospital the next day, but I did not go in her room. No matter what they said, it was too traumatic for me after seeing my father laying in his hospital bed … alive … for the last time. She was released sometime later and won a lawsuit with the Coca Cola Company. I bathed her and clothed her for a month or so until she was fully healed. She was never the same when she rode in the passenger seat of a car. She would jump at a sudden stop or someone blowing a car horn. She told me that when she saw the Coca Cola truck coming, she put herself under the dashboard and that's what saved her life. She had me laughing as she told the story of them laying her on the ground and covering her face to blow glass off her. She said as the air would blow, her dress would fly up and every time, she did that they told her not to move. She told them, "I am not going to let everyone see my panties; I am a lady."

My oldest brother had gotten bad on smoking crack. One time I remember him buying a new pair of shoes and selling them at the dope house. A few days later, after all his money was spent, he walked home in the middle of the summer in Phoenix wearing only socks. We asked him what had happened to his shoes. He told us that they tore up. Well, a few hours later there was a knock on the door and a man came to give my brother back his shoes. He said, "I felt so bad for him that I bought them back for him." My brother was embarrassed to say the least. There was another time when he asked to borrow mom's car, and she said yes. She had one of those old school cars that were made of metal. Well, when he brought the car back, we had to take the clothes to the laundromat. I attempted to open the trunk and sit the clothes basket on the bumper but the basket kept falling. I noticed then that the bumper was missing. He had sold the bumper at the scrap yard. We laughed for days about that, and even now that memory makes us laugh! It is one of those funny, not funny moments, but crack is no joke. This drug can and will have you doing things that you never thought you'd do.

LifeScript 3

More Than One Addiction

As the years continued to seem to fly by, my abuse and need for my drug of choice "DOC" became evident to me and my mother as well as my children. I soon went back to day labor where I worked weekly driving rental cars to and from the airport at Sky Harbor in Phoenix. Throughout it all, I felt like I was made for more. I was always looking for a man like my father: strong and dependable, Indeed, I am still searching for that man with my father's characteristics. As my addiction and my need for the street life increased, the more I wandered from home. I was hanging out more on Buckeye Road where the Motorcycle Club was. It opened at midnight. My girls and I would start on Thursday finding out what we would wear for Saturday. When Saturday came, we would take a nap in the daytime, drop the kids off at our parents around 5 pm, and come back to my house or one of their houses. A few of my homegirls used PCP and some marijuana; for me, it was marijuana and crack cocaine. The one time I did take a puff of PCP, I said never again. That was a real trip!

We were driving over an overpass and the hood of the car we were driving in flew up. Before that happened, it had seemed we were driving slower than the other vehicles. We were driving a "Deuce and a Quarter" at that time. We all screamed and then we began laughing. As we continued, looking between the end of the hood and the dashboard trying to steer the car, we drove until we were able to pull over. We laughed so hard my homegirl wet her pants. We pulled over and tied the hood down.

As I look back at the close calls and incidents that I had; I know that God was with me and had a plan all that time for me. Back to the club, we would get ready by getting our minds ready (or so we thought). We would roll a huge blunt, a huge cigar emptied of tobacco and replaced with marijuana, and dipped in honey to seal it. We all had our own bottles of MD 20/20, saladitos and our strong drink for the road. Around 11:30 pm, we would load up, light up the Blunt, and push play on the car stereo. Snoop Dog's Song, "Gin and Juice" gave us the idea. When we stepped out of the car, all you could see was smoke, like his video "Gin and Juice." There was never enough gin and juice, but there was always plenty of smoke.

I'd often take my children swimming at the pool in our complex. One day a man walked up to the swimming pool and asked me for something to eat. Of course, I wanted to know who he was. When you are slanging dope, you want to know all the new faces in the hood. You never know; you might be entertaining a snitch. There's a saying, "Keep your friends close and your enemies closer." Well, I must have been bitten by the crush bug. I became closer to him, so close we started having "relations." I started noticing that he would only creep around at night after two months of us hanging out. I thought maybe since he was slanging too, he wanted to stay under the wire. We had new people on the block; they were Jamaicans. It became eerie at times; so much I had to bring my piece with me.

My homegirls and I had somewhat of a tradition. We would get together late Friday evening to play spades and dominoes. My Mother would join us a lot, but we did not drink or smoke in front of her. She knew this so she played a game or two and left. She knew how to play some dominos. I have witnessed her putting a can of "whoop-but" on some of the biggest dope dealers in town. Of course she did not know what their professions were. She would step out of the house and grab a seat, or she would say in the background what they should have played after that hand was up.

One day she stayed in as it was a record 124 degrees in Phoenix. We had a swamp cooler; it was too hot to stay inside and too hot to swim so we gathered outside under the tree and set up our game tables. Oddly enough, I had not seen my "man-friend" around for two months. Well, one Friday as it began to cool off, he walked up, out of nowhere, as we were playing dominos. He was acting like nothing had happened, so I began to feed him with a long-handled spoon. Two Fridays passed, and he was missing in action again. So, the next time he walked up, I pulled him to the side and asked him questions. That's when I found out he had a baby and a baby momma. He also shared that he had begun slanging for the Jamaicans.

One Thursday I had to go to the Jamaicans to re-up. It was scary to me because you never know what they're saying when speaking in their own language. I went in and they asked me, "Have I seen him?" I said "No." The thought never came to my mind about how they knew I knew him. I got my package and left.

The next day was Friday and we began to set up tables and cards from the store. Everyone who played had to bring their own bottle. That was the rule and everyone who played at my tables knew this. So, when he showed up, I was buzzing, kicking butt and winning money at the tables. He sat down next to me smelling like "who did it and what for." He took it upon himself to pick up my 40oz of Mickeys! Number one, he has never had it like that. Number two, my children's Fathers did not have it like that! Who in the world did he think he was? I warned him! "If you reach for my bottle again, you will lose a finger!" He said, "Okay now baby you know I need this." One of my new homies was sitting opposite me and said, "Well, you should have brought your own. Aren't you slanging for the Jamaicans? You should have it going on my brother. As a matter of fact, the times you have been at this table, I think you owe everyone at this table a little something-something. You cannot keep showing up with your hands out. Also, that's my girl and if you pick up her drink I bought, it's going to be a problem." So, he got up and left. Time went by and my new boyfriend left and he came back with beer, etc. He was not there thirty minutes and four Jamaicans walked up, pulled out their semi-automatics and started shooting.

Our children were outside playing; the neighbors were outside. When those guns went off, repeatedly, I just knew I was dead. I always played with my back against my front door for this reason. My piece was hidden in the oleanders next to my front door and I just could not get to it. Kids were screaming. I called my kids' names but over the loud popping noise they could not hear me. When it stopped, I had fallen out of my chair onto my front door. I could not get it open to save my life. (Later I found out my Mom locked it when she heard the shots). My oldest daughter's Father heard what happened, since his child was outside. He told me they would be over in a few hours. He came, asked me some questions about the Jamaicans, who this new dude was, and what I knew about him. He told me to take the kids upstairs and not come down until I heard from him. Hours later, he told me he had a talk with them. The dude that I was with, that showed up here and there, ripped them off and they wanted to find him. Later, the Jamaicans came to my house and apologized. It was at that time they told me that they were shooting with blanks. I told him it did not matter; it was the principle of the matter. This was not the streets or jungles of Jamaica. You cannot come in the hood and do some crazy *%&* like that! He told me he likes a woman who speaks her mind. We became friends. The hood was in an uproar for a while, and then it calmed down.

Across the way, over a large brick wall was an apartment complex. I had never ventured over there. A couple of my homegirls got caught up and did some serious time in prison. One evening I walked over and immediately found three small girls playing in the driveway. I asked where their mother was. They immediately said she was "cleaning." I knew what that meant: she was in the house getting high and wanted to get high in peace and let them out to play. These three girls were no older than five years old.

I proceeded to knock on the door. It took a minute for her to look out the peephole, and she opened the arcadia door instead of the front door. She asked me who I was. I told her I was a neighbor concerned for her children that were playing in the driveway area. She then opened the door and yelled at them to come in the house. When she opened the door, the house was in disarray and had the smell of cigarette smoke and old shoes. The girls came running in and she yelled, "How did you get out of the patio area?" The oldest said, "We climbed over the wall and I helped the others over. We wanted to go play at the playground mamma. That's all." She told them to go to their rooms. As she opened the door earlier, I saw a crack pipe in her hands. I knew that she could be a potential client of mine as well as using her house as a trap house for potential business. The more I frequented that complex, the more customers I accumulated.

One day I was at home and my beeper went off. As I was walking to the pay phone, she yelled over the wall that she needed me to come to her house right away. It took me a while to get there, but when I arrived, the bedroom was full of people getting high, and her children were playing in the living room. As I walked back to the room, I attempted to do business with a gentleman that wanted more than what I had on me. After selling most of my stuff, I sat down to take me a hit and a drink. I smelled gas. I did not think anything of it at first, but I continued to smell it and it became stronger and stronger to me. As I got up to open the window, I announced, "Do you'll smell gas?" They said I was tripping. Okay, be that as it may but my women's intuition has kept me thus far so I left. As I was walking out of the house, I noticed the kids playing with the oven. I looked back and said to the oldest daughter she was too young to be playing with the oven. Well, she said to me in a sassy tone, "My momma lets me make toast for us" so I said to myself, "Go ahead."

I walked out going back to my side of the block. I am not sure how much later it was, but the sirens of the fire truck and ambulance caused me to feel some type of way. Later that night as I was sitting on top of my mother's car, a couple of tramps walked up and told me that her kids went to the hospital. I asked why? They said, "The kids were trying to make themselves toast and consumed too much gas. The stove did not turn on, so the oldest stuck her head in (laid halfway inside the oven) while the others did the same." My heart fell. I felt guilty because I should have done something, but what? The mother said she was coming when I left.

A few days later, I saw her walking down the street looking for her children. She did not look right. The word on the streets was that two of her children did not make it and the one that survived, the State took her. The hood was not the same for a while; and she certainly was not the same as she walked seemingly for days looking for her children. She was eventually taken to the State Sanitarium on 24th and Van Buren in Phoenix.

After that tragic event, I went back to the apartment complex. I had customers over there that would come to my house and I did not like them knowing where I stayed. I wanted to keep that separate from what I did in the streets. I met a young lady and her children who were outside. It was about 6 pm when the sun went down. That's when everyone came out of the house in the summer. I stopped and complimented her and her children. The next time I saw her was in the laundry room and we struck up a conversation about re-upping and who to get it from. I then began to drop by to see how she was doing. One evening, I met her mother who was to me one of the most down to earth women that I have ever met. And that stands to this day. She was married, and she loved her husband who worked hard and who eventually lost his eyesight and passed away some years later. She had a lot of friends, men friends, and she would take me driving with her almost everywhere. I met a lot of people and had established friendships. She taught me how to hit a crack pipe while steering the car with my knees. When she did this, I had just taken a hit and freaked out. I thought we were going to crash into something or drive off the road. She used to make fun of me when she did this. She knew that I did not like it when she did it and every time she promised she would not do it, she did it, and I never got used to it.

One day while at her daughter's house, I found out they had a nephew that lived across the way in the same complex. I met him for the first time, and he stole my heart. He was funny and his house was always clean. I met her brother as well and he became very attracted to me; so, attracted to me that when I moved to Tucson, he would drive down and visit. To this day I am not sure if she or her daughter knew that I was sleeping with their brother who was married. So, her brother was there, and she introduced me to a longtime family friend that was there as well. He eventually tried to come on to me and I shut him down. He began to hand out hits of crack cocaine when he visited, which seemed like more times than not. He would always attempt to pass me up and give everyone at the table dope but me, until she said that if he was not going to give everyone something at that table, don't give anything at all. Every time he did that, she would give me some of whatever she had.

One day he came over and she was not there. I was on my way out the door to get us some liquor when he showed up and offered me a ride. It was just to the corner and I was dreading going as the sun was going down. I accepted, and we began to laugh and talk. I thought to myself, he isn't that bad, but he was not the type that I would ever date or think about sleeping with. So, we made it back and my friend was there. He had to go somewhere far to pick up a package. He asked me to go with him. I agreed. We drove across town to Maryvale, picked up the package and I thought we were coming back. We stopped at a house and he told me he had to go in for a minute. I waited in the car and eventually he came out. When we made it back, of course they said we took too long and he shared we made a stop. That was the second time I was in his car and I made it back and he did not try anything so when he asked me to ride somewhere with him, I did not think about him trying anything. But when we pulled up to the Motel-6 on Van Buren Street, my heart was pounding. I thought to myself, "What are we doing here?" When I asked, he told me he was going to check to see if a friend was there, and he asked me if I wanted to come up. I figured it would be alright, since the friend would be there, and I had a plan to stand next to the door. Well, no one was there. It didn't dawn on me that he had a key to the room. I got really nervous and I was too scared at that time to move. He said, "Don't be nervous. Come sit down until my friend gets back. He owes me some money."

I reminded him that they were waiting for us back at the house. He said, "Oh he won't be long; he never leaves for a long period of time." We began to get high; he pulled out a bottle of liquor and gave me some. I did not drink it and he asked me, "What? Do you think you are too good to take something from me? Or do you like niggas like her brother." I got up and headed for the door. He grabbed me by my hair and threw me on the bed. I tried to scream, but he pulled out a knife and cut me with it and told me that I would never see my kids again if I even tried to scream again. I bit him and fought back as much as possible. He hit me with his fist; I just knew I would pass out. No one called the police. They were probably used to it as the hotel was on the main hoe stroll in Phoenix.

He tore my shirt so that my chest would show, and he tried to pull down my pants, but I crossed my legs so tight that he could not get in. He threatened and began slapping me repeatedly. I began to cry uncontrollably, telling him stop. He would not. He finally pulled my pants down and when he attempted to put a condom on, I ran for the door. Just then he threw the liquor bottle at me and I stopped to turn around. He pulled out a small pistol. I went back to the bed. He turned and slapped me in the face with the gun. He told me to lie down and I did, and he raped me.

It was almost like it did not happen or I was dreaming or something. How could he do this? How could I put myself in a position like this? I felt something run down my head into my eyes. Later, I realized it was blood. I was just lying there while he did his business. At that very moment, I felt dark inside. I felt dirty. When he was done, he told me, "Get up! Get yourself together and get the *&* out! If you tell anyone, remember I know where you live, and I know what time your children go to school and what school they go to."

I left the hotel, walking down Van Buren in the middle of the day. No one seemed to notice that I had blood running down my face. If they did, they dared not get into anyone's business. Maybe they thought I was a prostitute that just was beat up by her pimp. Just then a lady standing on the corner stopped me and gave me something to wipe my face with. She helped me cross the street and she gave me a pair of shades to hide my face. I made it to my house. My mother was there. I ran upstairs into the bathroom and turned on the shower. No matter how hot the shower was or how long I stayed in there or how many times I took a shower, I could not get clean enough. I did not eat for a week. My mother was worried about me. I slept all day for days at a time. I remember hearing my friend knock at the door asking for me and my mom told her that I was sick. She stayed for a while, but my mother did not let her upstairs with me. My mother told me, "It's gonna be alright whatever it is." Just then I felt something release on the inside, and I began to sob deeply.

I never went to that house again. I never told her what happened to me and I always had an eye on my kids. It was a long time before I let a man touch me. I developed a survival tactic of always being next to the door of any room. I never put my back against anyone, nor did I allow anyone to stand behind me. There is a certain men's cologne that triggers me. I hate Motel 6s to this day and I never drove down Van Buren again. That day out of all days, I didn't carry my gun, or my switchblade. But I did from then on!

My mom was talking about moving to Tucson, as she wanted to get out of Phoenix and be with her other children. Since everything was going wrong in my life, I pondered the idea of leaving. It was a scary idea, but I welcomed it. What would I be losing out on? I would have a chance to be sober, get a job and the fact that no one knew me was enticing. She eventually left. I'm not sure if I told my oldest daughter's father—Mr. will be his name—that I was leaving with his child, nor did I tell the other father ("It" will be his name). I thought to myself, "Why they would care? They never did anything for them anyway." And they never tried to purse their children. My oldest did eventually reside with her grandmother. While there she was able to see her father. On the other hand "it" never attempted to contact us to provide child support etc.

I left Phoenix a few months after my mother did and traveled to Tucson. Before leaving, I had a yard sale and sold everything in the house that I could. I left behind a lot of dishes, etc. I purchased the bus tickets, boarded the bus with one suitcase for my children and one for me. It was decided that me and the kids would stay with my niece. She had five children of her own. My kids and I shared a room with her boys. We slept on a mattress on the floor. The next week or so I began looking for work. It was crowded to say the least, but I was grateful to have a place for me and my children.

Tucson was a quiet place; it was almost like moving to the country. I soon obtained a job with Avis Car Rental; it was a very interesting job. I loved it. I paid my niece money for allowing me and my kids to stay, and saved money to move into my own place. I took the bus to the airport and on the way noticed an area of town where I knew there were drugs being sold, you can tell by the atmosphere, the people and the way the houses looked like in general. I would pay very close attention whenever the bus drove down South 6th Avenue, on the way to the Laos Center where I transferred to the bus going to the airport. Eventually, I was able to get a car but as I did not know my way around Tucson, I followed behind the bus for a few weeks until I learned my way to work and back home.

Soon I found a place to score as I left work one day. I decided to drive by and peep it out. I saw people slanging dope. I saw prostitutes, etc. Soon afterward, I stopped by and picked up a twenty–piece and took it to my niece's house and smoked it. I realized that her husband at that time smoked as well. I kept my job, went to work, worked overtime now since I had to pay rent and plus, I wanted my own sack to serve but did not know anyone like that in Tucson. As was the rule on the streets, they treated me like a snitch when I purchased anything being a new face on the block. They would ask what I needed, take the money and show me where to pick it up from. It could be in the mailbox, under a rock, etc. And you had to take whatever size it was; to them they did not want to risk handing anything to a snitch. Who wants to go to jail? No one! I did not care. It was like that for a while until one day the "Big Man" was there and took an interest in wanting to meet with me. When I would show up on the block, he would ask me to come in, and at times I would sit for a while and he would ask me questions to get to know me. After a while, based on the way I looked and talked, he knew that I was not a snitch. He was from Phoenix as well, the West Side 19 Ave and Buckeye. We shared stories on who died, got shot and locked up, etc.

As time went on, so did my substance abuse. I left my job at Avis Car Rental and began working for Airport Car Shuttle and Budget Car Shuttle. It was good money and the tips kept me with a stash at home. My children were getting older. My oldest daughter began acting out at school, and at home. For the summers, she visited her Grandmother in Phoenix. The whole idea of that was so she could spend time with her Dad although I am not sure how much of that she did as he was still into the street life. I began to use more and more and more. The more I smoked crack cocaine, the more I wanted and the harder I worked for it. It never dawned on me that I had a problem with drugs at this time in my life. Every one of my siblings used drugs, drank, abused prescription pain pills, heroin, prostituted, etc. so, who was going to tell me to slow down or have a serious talk with me when they have a problem themselves?

As time went by, I moved closer to the airport so that I did not have to take the bus so far to work. I had lost my car as it broke down and I did not have the money to repair it. At that time the buses went on strike. Every day, five days a week, I walked from Valencia to the airport. I am not sure how many miles it was, but I walked. My oldest daughter became a latch key kid at an early age. We came up with a plan that she would barricade the door and let no one in. When they arrived home from school, they would get something to barricade the door with. I always made their meals the night before and she would microwave it and they would eat. As I look back, I am so glad nothing happened to my children as they stayed home while I worked. I had no money for a babysitter and no way to get them to my Mother's. My mother, sister and her baby's father moved in the apartment complex that I lived in on Valencia later on. At that time, he was slanging dope and other things. When I got paid, he was right around the corner, so it was convenient for me to call him and ask him to be at my mom's when I got off. I don't know when he began to smoke crack himself, but I found out when he came to my house one day early in the morning. I asked him what he wanted. He said, "I want to give you something." He was acting weird. He pulled out a huge sack of dope. He gave me some and he pulled out his paraphernalia pipe and began to hit it. Over the years, I had seen people trip out after they hit the pipe, but he won the prize hands down. He began to scream that rats were all over him. He began to barricade my door and look out my window constantly and get knives out of my drawers in the kitchen and hide them in his back pocket. I told him to finish up and get the *^&* out of my house before I called my sister. He handed me his whole sack and said, "You can have it. Just let me stay and get high." I told him it isn't worth it, so he left. The next time he came over, he looked like he had been up all night. I put him out again and down the street he ran. There was rumor put out in my family that I slept with him. That is a lie and whoever started that lie and told that lie to my kids should be ashamed of themselves. He was getting high and did not want my sister and his son to know it. I only found out this lie as someone in the family said something smart to me and that came out or their lying mouth. How do you live up to a family lie? Well you do not need to defend yourself that's for sure. The lie is still out today. I do not know who started it, but to this day I have a good reason to believe my sister "Stoney" did.

As life continued for me, my children got bigger and my oldest daughter became more curious about what I was doing in my room and the change to my behavior when I came out. She began to check every space that I left to see what I had left behind. The nosier she became, the more anxious I got and the more I began to get careless. At times when they would be in their rooms, I would have a drink and take a hit of my crack pipe. They would start fighting and up I go to check on them while rushing, stuffing the crack pipe down in the sofa and at times I would forget where I put it. When all was calm, and I began to check the sofa she would ask what I was looking for and at times I had to stop her as she began to help me. She would get mad of course thinking that I did not want her to help me, while all along I did not want her to find my paraphernalia. As time went by, eventually she did.

LifeScript 4

PARENTING: OR THE LACK THEREOF

My Father is dead. My Mom never parented me. I am a young parent with no guidance, and an addiction on top of that. Nevertheless, I loved my children. I worked hard as a single parent to fight and keep my children, by working and doing the best that I could, but again with no guidance. My lack is now lack that my children experienced. My oldest was determined to act out and always get her way. The more she acted out, the more I became anxious. I never knew what she was going to do; it was more than her wanting to be with her Father. I began to believe there was something mentally wrong with her. As time went by, her behavior became worse.

She continued to act out in school. I remember a time when her principal called me to come down to the school to meet with her. The principal began to explain that when a student in her class has a birthday, she would usually celebrate by asking the class to participate in singing happy birthday and signing a card. I believe it was my daughter's first time in her classroom. She was around eight or nine years old. Nevertheless, when it came to singing happy birthday, my daughter refused. When the teacher began to ask her to do it, she told her, "If you make me sing happy birthday, I will call the police and tell them you hit me and put this mark on my arm." I was floored to say the least. My first thoughts were "What the what?! And where did she learn this from? What is wrong with my child?" I knew early on that she was jealous of my other two children as she claimed many times that I loved them more. It's natural for children to do this and I attempted to give all my children the same attention. But this was not the case as she was getting all the attention. The principal shared in all her years she had never had this happen before so naturally her first instinct was to call the parent(s) so that they could shed some light on it.

Well, I attempted to explain her need for attention, but that will only get you so far. I felt as if they were blaming me. I'm not sure if she came home with me that day as it would have made sense for her not to go back in that classroom again after the threat she made. When she did things like that, I would call her grandmother in Phoenix who would not believe that her granddaughter would do anything like that. Well, she did.

There was another time she boarded the school bus and when the bus was in traffic she stood up and attempted to open the door of the school bus and jump out in traffic. The bus driver had to pull over and call the police. When he/she did, my daughter jumped off the bus and the police came knocking on my door.

When her behavior worsened, I decided to take two days off in the week and work weekends. One day, she didn't come home at her usual time and I panicked and called the police. They established a team of people to look for her, and I was told not to leave the house as she might show up. Well she sure did; she walked right up to the door as if nothing had happened, so I called the police back to the house. If you could have seen the look on her face and the behavior she portrayed, she could've won an Emmy Award that day and they fell for it. I knew then I was in big trouble. She claimed that the driver of the bus had been mean to her and did not like her. I am not sure if that driver lost his/ her job, but they did not drive for that district any longer. Months later we moved to South Sixth Avenue. I was approved for my Section 8 in that area. Usually a person with Section 8 housing can move anywhere in the United States, but when you lose it you must start all over again. This was another way God provided as I look back.

As time went on, she did more things, and it became unbearable. She would call the police and tell them I did not feed her, or that I spanked her with a belt. I owned up to the belt spanking, but when she said I did not feed her and made her sleep outside that was a bold-faced lie. Nevertheless, Child Protective Services (CPS) got involved and boy was I *&^ off. I said to myself if I did not feed my child, she would not be the size that she is now, and the other two children can testify to the lack of feedings if ever there was a time. If anything, I went without food so that they could eat. Why would I not feed her and feed the other children? CPS can kiss my A** and I told them that. My goal for this book was not to curse, but when I think about the mess I went through with her, it still floors me to this day. When I look back, I truly believe she did all of this to get away from me and be with her Father who was never around and had several babies across Phoenix. She wanted to go where they would let her get away with anything. Again, her grandmother did not believe that I was telling the truth about her behavior.

She came home crying one day as she walked home from school. I asked why. She claimed that a man was following her. With her numerous calls to the police, you can expect that I'd become acquainted with them. Anyway, I called them, and they came out and set up a sting to where they would follow her to school in plain, unmarked cars. They would have unmarked cars strategically placed on the side of the roads to watch cars that would stand out. They would leave when she got to school and be there at the school and their spots when she left and walked home. The goal was to do this so that they could catch a pattern for the car that was following her. Of course, I was terrified that something might happen. After a week's investigation they met with me and her and shared what they found. Nothing! They began to ask her was this truth in the first place, and they began to explain to her the man hours it took and the people who really needed their help at that time who did not get the help that they needed right away because they put all their manpower into catching this person. They began to speak and explain to her the differences and consequences of false reporting. She got up off the sofa and walked in her bedroom.

Time went by and she began to call the police on me while I was in the kitchen cooking or something, for no reason at all. I could be doing laundry, etc. I remember a time when she was under their bunk bed screaming, at the tops of her lungs, and she did not want to come out. I tried my best to calm her down and by offering her things to no avail. The police came and he even got down on the floor and tried to get her to come out. Eventually she did. They asked her what was going on and why she called the police. She had no reason, no excuse, it's just that she wanted to. They spoke to her again and warned her that if she called them again, they would lock her up in a jail for young ladies. Well, she did, and they did. A week or so after she arrived home, she called the police again. The police came and told her that she did not know how good she had it. He told her that children a few houses down did not have plates to eat from, a sofa to sit on, and she was complaining about what her Mom was cooking. She just rolled her big eyes.

As time went by, CPS got involved again. This time she was making claims again of me beating them with a belt and starving them. CPS visited the school and talked with the two youngest separately. When I found out, I was mad as *&^ ! The only thing I was trying to hide was that I was on drugs. No matter what, I loved my children. Yes, I had a drug problem, but so did most of the single mothers, widows, married people, businessmen and women in the world. I did the best that I could as a single mother with no positive role models in my life. It was what it is.

I did not have the same problems with my other two children. It was always the oldest. I tried to give her the attention she desired, but I stopped that because it was never enough. She wanted more and more, and I had two other children that needed my attention as well. They had her on medications that worked when she took them. It was like having my baby back: no fits, no outbursts. She was cooperative, and she did what I asked her to do and more. But soon she stopped taking them as she saw the difference in her behavior as well.

Later, we met a Pastor from her school who oversaw the African-American Studies program and had his own church. They would go and study and learn the names in the Bible and I was able to get some peace. Years later; I would be attending that church and teaching Sunday school and my mother would be the mother of the church.

Eventually, we found ourselves in court. It had been a long road and I was tired and worn out. It was evident she did not want to go back home with me and after all of this I was tired and wanted her to go! I couldn't help but think, "You want to get away from me that bad then go!" I was given the choice of giving the state guardianship until she was eighteen. I gave up guardianship, and it felt like a piece of my soul left. As I signed the papers, my hands were shaking. As I looked up at my daughter; she had a grin on her face that I can see to this day. She went to a group home. She complained and complained and said she wanted to come home. She'd call me crying, "Mama, I am sorry. I will be good. Please can I come back?" I told her, "No, you made your bed; now you have to sleep in it. You belong to the state now, but if you truly want to come back, we can talk with your social worker and see what she has to say." The last group home she went to, she could not get her way. She jumped on one of the workers, took her money and ran to my house. When she told me what she had done, I told her to take the money back before they locked her up for real.

Eventually she came back to my home, but it wasn't that long before I sent her to her Grandmother in Phoenix. Her Grandmother and I were on good terms until I did this. She was angry at me to say the least. It's not what I did, but how I did it. I put her on the bus with her clothes, money and a note for her Grandmother. I had had it at that point and felt somebody else should see what I was going through. Years later, her Grandmother called me to apologize. She told me that I was so angry at you and what you did I could not see straight. She came down here, lied about you and what you were doing and I believed it, until I got a taste of what she was like with you. Her Grandmother began sharing with me that one time my daughter left for school before her Granny went to work. Her Granny got a call from the school about their dress code and what my daughter came to school dressed in. She got there and saw that her granddaughter had on one of her skirts, make-up and a short blouse. She took her home and spoke very honestly to her. She told her, "It's not your mama. Well, maybe she did some things wrong, but you played a huge part in it as well. She saw what I had experienced. Finally, I got peace that it was nothing that I did or didn't do; it was her behavior and attitude.

My son had issues as well, with stopping up the toilets at school with paper towels. He had trouble on the bus as well, but nothing like what I went through with my oldest child. My youngest daughter was very talented and exceeded in everything she put her mind to: jazz dance, purse making classes that used beads, etc. She was tested for the gifted program and accepted, but I allowed her to make the decision if she wanted to go or not. She did not so I asked her why. She said, "Mama, those are the kids we make fun of."

Time went by and eventually I went back to work at the airport. I started working for Hertz Car Rental at that time and I am going to tell you what went down only because it's in the past and restitution was paid back. I did time and it's over even though they never caught my niece who was a huge part in this as well. Anyway, working at Hertz Car Rental as a driver we would go to different places delivering cars, picking up cars and transporting cars from the airport to the main site during our busy hours. It was at that job I met a young Mexican man and we messed around for a bit. I never brought numerous men in and out of my house; all my children can testify to this. Either we would hang out at his house or he would do some midnight creeping "bootie call" at my house while the children were asleep. He was the only one that I allowed to do this as we had to keep it on the down low working at that same job. I know that I liked him a lot and vice versa but he had a crazy baby momma.

One day I was driving a car from the airport to the lot and I heard something thump in the back seat. When I arrived at the lot, I looked and it was a day planner filled with credit cards. I wanted to turn it in to lost and found but that did not happen. I hid it and when I left for the day, I put it in my lunch bag. When I got far enough from the job, I looked inside and there were credit cards for almost every store there is. So I decided to try one. I went to Circle K and used one to fill my gas tank. I was so scared that I did not stand there too long. I thought everybody and their mamma was looking at me. To be completely honest, I almost wet my pants. However, when I saw that I could get away with that, I tried using that same card to purchase things from small gas stations and eventually shopping online. It had been a month and I had to keep that job so that I could get a heads-up if anything was going to go down. The last store that I shopped at was Victoria's Secret.

I told my niece about it and she shopped at Target and she got her car repaired and other things and shortly afterwards she moved to Texas. One day I was walking home from one of the neighborhood stores and some of the dope houses attempting to sell some goods that I had. As I looked up, I saw unmarked police cars in front of my house. When I got closer, I saw one of the black police officers that worked as Airport Police standing at the car door. I knew right then and there, I was busted. But I did not want to give anything away just yet before I had spoken with them. And i7 just so happened I had some Victoria Secret body spray on me as well as dope so I had to play it cool. I knew that I had to keep my wits so that they would not be suspicious and besides if they were going to arrest me there would have been a police car there. Anyway, I walked right by them as if I did not see them. I knew that I had to get in the house and put my dope up and not only that my stolen products. As I passed them up, they called out my name, but I kept going.

As I said, I had one thing in mind, well two, getting inside the house and throwing my dope out of my hand behind something. And since the other person looked like an investigator that meant they came to ask me questions. They knew nothing; they were fishing. I thought it was funny when they assumed this was a ring of thieves. Either he was just being naive or bucking for a promotion. He went on to say that I was the little fish they needed to get to the big fish. What he did not know at that time though was I was the big fish. However, this was not a huge ring of bandits; it was just an opportunity that I took advantage of.

They proceeded to show me a video of a lady and my niece at Target shopping and at other stores with the victim's credit card. My niece even went as far as finding a crackhead who vaguely resembled the lady on the credit card. I told them I did not know who the other lady was. I started thinking about what my niece had done. That video showed them going into the store and using the same cashier each time. Now common sense says that if you come through three times purchasing large items something may be wrong. I said, "Speak to the cashier who allowed this. Maybe they paid her something." The detective said, "Well, she was actually the fraud detection cashier and unfortunately she was fired. Somehow thieves usually use the last checkout station in a store."

Again, I asked, "Why you are here?" The airport police officer said, "Ms. Gonzales, it seems that you are on video at Circle K using one of the credit cards to purchase gas. And being that you worked for Hertz at that time, we knew this was you we just need to find the other lady." It was my niece and I did not want to say anything. To this day, they have not done anything to her because the victim was paid off by me and I did all the time.

After they left, I knew I was in big trouble. As time went on, they gave me a chance to turn myself in seeing that I asked them to give me time to take care of my personal business, including taking care of my children, closing up my house and getting high as a kite before I turned myself in. While I was in jail, I had a public defender who at first sight reminded me of Colombo, complete with wrinkled suit and disheveled hair. The only difference was he was young. The guards escorted me to my visit. I was shackled to the table and the guard waited outside the see-through room. The Public Defender then handed me a stack of evidence they had on me and the ten-year stretch I was looking at not withholding the restitution to the victim. I asked him, "What you are going to do about this?" He said, "If you give us the name of the other two women, I can get you off on probation with fines seeing that this is your first charge of this magnitude. You will also go home, released on your own recognizance, while you await trial." Eventually I gave up my niece's name after hearing the time I was looking at. He warned me that the State's Attorneys were brutal. "They are going to paint a picture of a single mother with no education and low income looking for an easy escape on someone's else's dime."

LifeScript 5

THE FISH BOWL

Well, it was time to go to court. I was transported to the Supreme Court's downstairs jail via van. Before you enter the van, which had no windows, all inmates had to be shaken down for weapons, shackled from ankle to ankle and hand to hand while shackling you to the next person behind you. We were strategically placed by the inmate's court dates and where they were going inside of the courtroom. Once everyone was shackled, they are led inside of the van by the first shackled inmate. If someone fell, we would all fall, and when you entered you could not sit down until they gave you permission. Then the Correctional Officers shackled you to the floor of the van as well.

I was preparing myself for ten years, as this was just the first hearing and there would be several more. When it came down to sentencing me, I was scared to say the least; I did not want to see the inside of a prison. As we began to talk in the holding tank, a few of us had the same judge. The frequent flyers were saying this was a good judge and that somehow eased my fear. As they called our names, the doors opened to the holding cell and we were shackled together again, taken up in the elevator through the back hallway and into the courtroom. My sister "Stoney" and the Pastor were there as I was the last one to be called by the judge. He asked me to stand as he was talking. Looking back, I believe that I disassociated for a minute or two as I did not hear much. It was almost like I was there but not there. He started by telling me "because this was my first serious charge ..." and asked if I had anything to say. I said, "No." He proceeded sentencing me to one hundred and eleven days at the Pima County Minimum Security Facility on Mission Road. I could not believe it! I had three felonies and on top of that now I had an alias. I cried like a baby.

Looking back, I see that God's hands were all over my life. While there, I did not complain one day, although I was put in lock down a couple of times. It was very embarrassing, but it was what I needed. They called it the "Fishbowl." It was a huge circled wall of glass, and when you were put in there, you traded your maroon outfit for a yellow one, therefore resembling fish inside of a fishbowl. I was in there a week until the head Correctional Officer of that unit or whoever decided it was time for me to come out. There were perks about being in there. You didn't have to worry about someone walking up on you and you didn't have to stand in line for chow.

I remember a church frequently visited. One day they came to baptize. I wanted to get baptized because everyone was making a big deal out of it but did not know at that time what it meant. Now I know the significance of it. There was talent in there. There were women who could decorate your envelopes with pictures of cartoon characters for your children or whoever. They used tampons and other things to design the envelopes. The women who had this talent as well as French braiding hair did this as they did not have anyone on the outside to put money on their books to purchase commissary items. By the way, if they would have gotten caught using an object for something other than what it was intended for, they would have been in serious trouble for that is called contraband.

I was so lonely in there. I felt as if I did not have anyone on the outside that cared to even come and visit me. I knew that my Mother may have, but she had both kids at that time. I did get a chance to call her as she had gotten sick and one of the guards allowed me to make a 10-minute call from their desk. She told me not to worry about her and the kids but to take care of myself. I had also allowed my Mother to take my checks and pay my rent so that I could have a place to go to after I was released. I eventually was released, and I went to my Mother's house. She had been cooking and it smelled good. While there, my oldest sister Mary was released from SACRC prison. My mother had allowed her to stay home and get high. That way she could keep an eye on her. She knew that if she did not, Mary would not have taken her medications (insulin) and wind up in the hospital again

LifeScript 6

THE URGE TO STAY THE SAME

As usual, they were getting high. Although my mother allowed it, she had rules. No one was to come over after midnight, and if someone was still there, they had to leave. My sister abided by the rules.

I had a chance to be with my children. I had called Section 8 and asked to move. I did not want anything else from that duplex I was living in. I wanted a new start for me and my two children. I moved into a home still in the zoning area of South Tucson. I had started using again. I met an older man at a Walgreens one day. He was tall and thin. Let's call him Shorty. He was slick and smooth, so I thought. He followed me out of Walgreens and asked for my number and I gave it to him. We started dating shortly afterwards. I would bring him to the house, where he would play games with my kids and they loved him. Our relationship took a turn for the worst when we began to get high together. Everyone I knew on the south side was shocked that I was with him, but I did not see anything wrong with him. Years into the relationship, I began to hear stories of him beating women. I did not see that, and I did not believe it. Years went by before I realized what people told me was true.

One day Shorty came to my house mad. I was in the kitchen cleaning and he asked me something and I had a sarcastic attitude about it. As I walked through the living room, he jumped in front of me and slapped the mess out of me. I was shocked! Just then I remembered all the things that I had been told. Shorty apologized, but the beatings became more frequent and so did the apologies. I had to call the police on Shorty many times. But as usual he would leave, and they could not do anything about it if he was not there.

There was a time when I was at my Mother's house and she needed water. Shorty volunteered to go, but I was the only one with a car. So, for him to prove that he would come back he took my son with him. I did not think that he would do anything wrong with my son and he didn't because he dropped my son and the jug of water off and left. I did not see him for another week. He pulled up to my Mother's house high as a kite. I went outside to get my keys back. He gave them to me and then forced me to take him to his sister's house. Well, I did it just to get rid of him. While we were in the car, he began cursing at me and threatening me. I was so fed up; I had enough at this point. Not only was he cursing at me, he began to brag about how many women he slept with in my car, etc. I did nothing, and just stayed calm; my focus was on dropping him off at the police station downtown with a little Pomp and Circumstance!

As we turned the corner on Broadway to Stone, he yelled, "Why the **&^ are you going this way?" I did not say anything, but sped up as the car began overheating. When we arrived at the police station, I made him think I was going to pass by but pulled in the police station's parking lot and laid down on the horn. My passenger side door would not open unless you rolled the window down and stuck your hand out of the window to open it. Well, I locked it from my side of the car. I did not stop blowing that horn. He kept saying, "You let me out of here or I will kick your *^&% you *#$%^." I said, "Do it! You worthless piece of ***!!!" Just then an officer came out of the police station. Shorty jumped over the back seat dropping one of his shoes in the front seat. I yelled, "Who's the loser now you sorry excuse of a man." Well, I said something else but use your imagination. Anyway, he made it across the street and hid behind a garbage can. A police officer came out and asked if anything was wrong. I told him my car was overheating and for some weird reason my horn began to blow. He asked me for my license and registration. I handed it over as I was legit. I drove off and passed him up walking to his sister's house ... with one shoe in his hands. As I passed him up, I blew the horn and waved at him with his shoe. I laughed all the way home and so did my family when I told them what I had done.

I had not seen him in a month, until he knocked on my door one day. I let him in. My probation officer was just driving by that day, so she said, and saw him coming into my home. I was just on regular probation at that time. I believe they were watching me all long. After he was in, I heard a knock; I was surprised to see her. She called me outside and asked if anyone was in there with me. I said no, as by that time he had snuck out the back door and jumped the fence. Another plain clothes PO drove up and proceeded to search my house. She told me, "I know that Shorty was in here. He's a dangerous man and you are not allowed to be with him or anyone with a criminal background." Eventually, I was put on IPS (Intensive Probation Service) even though I was on regular probation after being released the last time I kept messing up. I kept using drugs and missing my scheduled days to do a UA. I called and told her that I could not do probation any longer; I wanted to turn myself in as I knew if they caught me with dirty urine I would do the full stretch of the ten year sentence. Because, they did not do an UA on me when I turned myself in, the judge at that time sentenced me again to a month in jail.

I partied before I went to jail this time and sold everything in my house. When I was released, I stayed with my Mother. I did more partying than ever at that time, but I began to look at my mistakes, the things that I did not do and the lack of parenting because I stayed high. Around that time, my Mom had a pacemaker put in. I was not aware of this until a month or so later. I knew she was in the hospital, but did not know how serious it was.

Sometime after she got out, she was doing well but was always having problems with her pacemaker shifting and not working properly. I remember her telling me it gave her a lot of problems. After that surgery, I noticed

something changed. She was always looking around as if to pay close attention to the beauty of God's handiwork. Leading up to my Mother's passing, she had moved. She was always moving because of issues that came
with allowing so much traffic through her house. That time would be her
last move.

I hadn't seen my sister Mary in a while and when I arrived at my Mother's, I went to Mary's room as usual and she was in there along with four or
five other people. My Mother would always knock on Mary's door to make
sure she was taking her insulin and eating. Mary was happy to see me, and
she had just picked up some dope so she told me to come and sit on the bed
with her and I did. She began to give me dope to smoke. My sister Squeaky
was in the corner in a chair and she kept saying, "What about me Mary?"
Mary would of course give her a hit or two, but Squeaky got tired of asking. As usual Mary would doze off and there would always be someone in
the room watching her to make sure she was alright and that no one stole
from her, which they wouldn't dare, or so I thought. At that Mary dozed off
again and at that time Squeaky sat on the edge of the bed next to the wall
so her view was Mary's back. I was sitting next to Mary on the bed and I
then took the chair in front of the bed, so that I could be more comfortable.

Mary dozed off again, but I was not watching for her dope and where
she put it. I would never take anything from her; she has always looked
out for me and protected me on the streets. After about twenty minutes,
Squeaky said she would be back. Squeaky always stayed close to Mamma,
either in the same apartment complex or down the street. Squeaky was
gone for about an hour. When she came back, Mary had awakened. As
usual she woke up looking for what she had in her hand, dope or crack
pipe. She found her pipe, but she did not find her dope. The first thing that
came to my mind was, if they do not find it, she will blame me for it seeing that I was the only one close to her and on the bed before she went to
sleep. Mary began arguing with me; Momma came in the room and told
us to be quiet. I left out of the house because I knew the doctor told her

that she needed to be in somewhat of a quiet atmosphere. As I was walking out, the other people in the bedroom left as well. Of course, Squeaky stayed in the room. As I came back in the house, I did not go in the bedroom; I knew that Mary was still mad. One of Squeaky's friends that she got high with came in and asked for her. I told her that it was not a good time. This is when she called me outside and told me to tell Mary she did not know that it was her stuff that Squeaky had. "What" I asked her. She proceeded to say that Squeaky got high with her and she did not know where it came from. She continued by saying, "I was just told that someone took Mary's stuff and knowing that Squeaky never has anything, I knew right away what happened." To say the least, I was furious! I was set up.

My Mom kept attempting to quiet Mary down. As she left out of her room, Momma went in the bathroom gripping her chest. I asked was she alright. The look on her face said different as she shook her head yes. I called 911. Mary was told that the ambulance was coming but she never left her room. As I was waiting with my Mom in the living room, she stood up. I could hear the sirens in the background, but they sounded so far away even as they seemed to get closer. I ran back in the living room, watching over mama at that time, but I had to leave to see if I could spot the ambulance as it was nighttime.

They were at the wrong house down the street. I yelled, and I yelled. I ran in the house and yelled for someone to run down there to get them. As I was walking back out to see if they were coming, Momma was sitting on the sofa; she had this look in her eyes. She stood up and grabbed her throat as if attempting to say something. I yelled, "Momma, what is it? She reached out to me. Just then the sound of the ambulance was finally close and loud. I ran out to let them in and as soon as I turned to go out of the door, I heard a loud thump. I found out later that Momma had fell to the floor and hit her head on the side of the table.

As they were working on her, Squeaky and I were getting ready to follow behind them. But it took them a while to leave the house. I kept saying to myself, "Why aren't they leaving?" We arrived at the hospital and they escorted me and Squeaky into a room. To this day, I don't remember what they said as my mind was somewhere else.

I am not sure who called Stoney, but she and her husband arrived shortly after Momma passed. I cried all the way out of the hospital, but not like my other sisters did. I asked myself, "What in the *%$ is wrong with me? Why am I not grieving like the rest of the family?" Yes, I was crying, and I was sad that I did not get to know her while she was here and that she's gone, but I did not grieve like them. This is the way I understand this, and it took me years to figure it out. It was not that I did not love my Mother. I did. But I did not fully know her as my other siblings did. She did not raise me; my Father did. They had spent more quality time with her than I did. So, it's natural for them to grieve differently than me. I pray this makes sense to whoever is reading this.

Sometime after the funeral, I began to hear a lie spurring around in the family. I had noticed family members saying things, snide remarks, but I did not think anything about it. First of all, I did not know what they meant, and I did not care because it did not pertain to me. However, it came out that I killed my mother!!! What!!! I could not believe this! At that moment, I was done with my family.

Squeaky left soon, I mean SOON after the funeral and moved to Texas where she is to this day. She should have. I was set up! But no one cared to ask me what happened. If I was on trial, I would have been found guilty. The circumstantial evidence was against me. I can't believe that even to this day she would continue to allow this to go on. Families have tendencies to let things go on for too long. Well now the cat is out of the bag. I am not saying this to get back at Squeaky, but I do believe that this lie has caused a rift in my relationship with my children to this day. I told my youngest daughter what happened, so she knows. What I want to know though is how a grown adult can inflict trauma on children like this. How could you tell my pre-teens that I killed their grandmother, whom they loved dearly?

She was like a Mother to them. Out of all the things that a person can do, telling a child this lie is so cruel.

After my Mom's passing, I frequented South Sixth Avenue. That was my stomping grounds. I had no place to call my own, and when I did, I lost it. I also lost control after that lie had been told. My habit now had taken control of me and I was wandering aimlessly. I was arrested numerous times for vagrancy, shoplifting and trespassing. Every week, one to three times a week, I was being arrested by the same cop. I would always appear before the same Judge, the Honorable Ronald Wilson. From January 2008 through July 2008, I was in and out of his courtroom, charged with giving false information to the police and criminal nuisance. Let me say something about the false information. It seemed like every week the same police officer arrested me. But he asked me my name every week so I told him my name was "Puddin-Tang." I yelled at him, "You arrest me almost every week. You patted me down on a regular basis, so much that you know the size of my breasts so, to ask me my name was in insult!" So that made him mad and he started adding charges that did not make sense: criminal trespassing, failure to obey and shoplifting. It had gotten so bad that I was banned from South Sixth Avenue. Did that stop me? No! I kept going back over there. They would arrest me when they saw me pretending to rest at the bus stop, knowing that I just needed to sleep and run me out of the area.

My habit had taken control of me. That's when I met a lady that was a member of Rising Star Baptist Church, may she rest in peace. She opened her home to me early in the morning when I would knock on her door. She'd make me a pallet on the floor, and I would fall right asleep. The next morning, she would fix me breakfast and talk with me about God. I showered and left again, creeping around corners hiding from the police.

My sister (Stoney) would allow me to come to her house for a few days, but that was like hell. If you are going to help someone, make sure you are doing it from your heart and not so the family and your friends think you're an angel. As she left with her husband to go to work, she also left her pitbull loose in the house. He was huge and mean and whenever I tried to step out of the bedroom to go use the bathroom, he would come running down the hallway or he would be sitting right by the door. I did not go very often to her house since I had experienced better treatment on the streets. She had married one of her tricks. He was a dentist she did not want me there too long. Being insecure, she felt she had to watch over her meal ticket. I will get into that later.

Back then, you needed a TB test to get into the Salvation Army and it took three days to be read. So, I stayed with her in the meantime. When I would get into the shelter, I tried my best to get back that same day and on time as otherwise the bed will be given away. They only allowed you a week's stay at a time so when that week was up, I was homeless again. There were a couple of occasions I slept in the park to stay close by the shelter so that I could get back in, have a hot meal and a place to stay. I remember having no plate to eat from, no utensils to eat with and pop-top cans were my best bet if I wanted to eat. I had an appointment with the social worker at the shelter who told me that I could stay, have my own room and pay a certain amount, and I would also be able to come in late, etc. Well, of course I took advantage of that. I got high there, snuck in late sometimes and for five months it was good until I caught up to me.

I would go back to South Sixth and hide out there for a few days. I was lucky when they did not catch me sneaking in, but eventually they caught me sneaking out. Back to jail I went. One day, I had court and Judge A. Wilson looked out and told me that he was sick and tired of seeing me in his courtroom. I thought, "What? After months of putting me in jail, now you see that's not working? Oh, and by the way your cops are crooked." That was the attitude I had towards him being an African-American Judge. I expected more from him. To be honest, I guess I expected him to let me go every time I went into his courtroom. I expected a free ride and not help. He can tell you the Hot Mess I was back then and, whenever he saw my name on the docket, wherever it was, he would put mine at the top to get me out of his courtroom quickly. When I spoke with him after court, I do not remember word for word what he said, but he did the best thing anyone had ever done for me up to that point. He sent me to Tucson Centers for Women and Children which is now named Emerge. He gave me the number and told me to call them. When I left, I was hungry and tired, but I just knew this was the right thing. I felt it! There was a company on the left-hand side—it was an insurance company or a notary—but I walked in and asked to use the phone and they allowed me.

They must have heard my conversation. After I got off the phone, these people prayed for me and gave me bus fare. I walked to the bus stop, and I arrived at the location they wanted me to meet them at. God had a hand over my life all that time. He guided the Judge to really help me and he made a way for me to get into that place.

LifeScript 7

THE BEGINNING OF A WONDERFUL CHANGE

After meeting with them at an undisclosed location, I was brought in, and given an intake or assessment. I was then shown around, but I really don't remember what they told me. I was mentally and physically tired, and I needed to rest. I was given the bottom bunk and was told that I could rest all I needed to. There were four bunks in that room, and I had one roommate who would read the Bible a lot. What I remember about that place is that it was full of women, which brought comfort to me as I was seeking other females who understood the struggles we were faced with out in the streets, who understood the need for peace, understanding, non-judgement and love.

I slept, ate, slept and ate. That went on for a week or so. My body was not used to sleeping in a bed, so my body would jump at times and I would sleepwalk. Not only was I not used to sleeping in a bed, I was not used to sleeping with both eyes shut, if you know what I mean. The times that I did get somewhat of a rest on the streets is when I had to sleep in a crack house, where you had to sleep with one eye open or have enough crack to pay someone to watch your stuff while you slept. Anyway, that was not so there. My room was next to the kitchen and there were days when I had awakened and went in for breakfast ate and went back to sleep. The cafeteria was always open but not the kitchen. There were always graham crackers, jelly, bread for toast, etc.

After a month of rest, I "awakened" and realized that I needed to make a choice, and my choice in 2008 was that I would never go back to Sixth Avenue and I would never smoke crack cocaine again. We were allowed three months max, but in some circumstances, you could stay more with a plan for your exit. If you were staying the three months or longer, you worked with your case manager to get the help that you needed. I came in with the clothes on my back, but there were always donated clothes. It was safe and comfortable there; this was one place my abuser would not be able to find me. They would never tell him where I was; I was safe from the outside world.

They had a TV room with lots of postings of jobs, housing, etc. There was also talk of a church that was paying the first ten or so people to clean up around the church cash money. It was a few hours on a Saturday, and I thought that would be perfect as I did not want to beg for another cigarette from the ladies there. So, I caught the bus to a Church in the community. It was a while before I met the Pastor—Pastor Chris Dehan. I would work for two or so hours, raking and cleaning up. It was a quick way for me to make some money and soon after I was done, I went to the nearest store, purchased my Newport Cigarettes and some snacks and headed back to the Center. I did this for a while and then they stopped offering it. I am not sure why.

I found a realty company that allowed felons to rent and gave second chances. Now, seeing that I knew what my background was, doubt came to my mind and I was filled with so much anxiety I wanted to run back to the streets. I had my mind made up that I was not going to get it. I left message after message for her to call me back. It was coming up on my two months there and I needed to get started on my exit plan and a new sober future. Fortunately, at that time they were undergoing a name change as well as moving locations so that gave me a little more time. When I arrived and settled in the new place, the manager called from the realty company. She was so nice, and I was able to get to know her and her staff as she gave me a chance and a new start in life. Now that I look back, I see another instance of God's hands all over my life: guiding me, protecting me and providing for me.

I met someone from the realtor's staff off site and they showed me where I would be living. It was nice—finally my own place. I was nervous to say the least. Arriving back at night, I noticed a young lady hanging outside late at night. That was not the first time I had been her. One night I saw her sitting in the far corner of the backyard and decided to go and see what was up. As I got closer, my suspicions were correct, she was getting high. I wanted some so she gave me a hit. From the first hit, I knew it was wrong. I did not have the taste for it and on top of that, it made me sick to my stomach.

Most of us kept the same bunkoes, but mine was leaving. It was always sad to see someone leave as you didn't know how or even if they would make it. As she was packing, she asked if she could trade Bibles with me. On the cover of her Bible was a picture of hands with broken chains around the wrists. I thought to myself, "I've been set free."

I had decided to go back to church and I eventually did. I began to attend church regularly where the pastor was the one I met from my daughter's school years before. I knew then that Tucson was a small place and that everybody knew everybody in the African-American Community. God does work in mysterious ways. I was able to teach Bible study there, attend church and get to know God and what He wanted me to know. For a while my sister (Mrs. Stoney) would drive me to and from while I was there at the center, as well as when I exited the program. When I moved into my own place, I eventually began attending the "family" church at times and attending Pastor Chris's church. I felt the move of the Spirit at both churches. I was being led by God, and this was no mistake. I was able to attend the women's retreat at Pastor Chris's church and it was beautiful. I met and became friends with members in the church. One day I received a ride home and to the grocery store from a beautiful couple who resided not too far from my home. While arriving at my home, she asked if she could help take grocery bags up for me. I did not want her to do this as she would notice my empty living room. The next Sunday they met with me after church and told me they had a sofa they wanted to get rid of and asked if I'd want it. "Of course" I replied, with tears welling in my eyes. They walked this sofa to my house and gave me silverware which I needed (this is another instance where God was taking care of me). I felt like I belonged there. The worship was different than I was used to. It was quiet at times. I needed to shout as God was speaking to me through songs and workshop, but I felt that I could not do that there, so back to the African-American Church I went.

I went back to the little storefront church and eventually developed a feeding ministry. I was able to go deliver food on the bus and had plenty left over for whoever was in need. I felt the Spirit of God moving me to leave the "family" church. I was spiritually growing faster than expected and God had a plan for me to continue growing. So, Shorty's sister, may she rest in peace, took me to the noonday Bible study at Rising Star Baptist Church, where the Senior Pastor is Amos L. Lewis. I loved it! The Word was being explained and I was being fed. I was missing that knowledge and the worship style. God and I knew that I would be able to grow there, but it was not my time to be there. With the help of the Holy Spirit, I was studying in the Spirit and in the knowledge of God; however, it was a slow process, a year and a half to be exact. These were years that He dealt with me and the strongholds that were still attached to me. He dealt with me in a season of studying, praying and learning the difference between God's voice and Satan's voice. He began pruning the bad fruit for the good fruit to show. I wanted to be free; I wanted Him to clean me up, I wanted to be with God, and I wanted to know who He was and what He wanted from me.

In between studying, one of my sisters in Christ, may she rest in peace, gave me a book called *Purpose Driven Life* as well as *Battlefield of the Mind*. I was so touched and felt the move of God and to know that I was loved and I was not a mistake. I also started to know that even though I was in a battle, the fight was fixed, and He had already won!

The process was hard to say the least as He began to show me things; one of them was my abuser. Yes, I let him back into my life when I was sober and newly saved. He came to my house, and we had sex. Why did I continue to go back? Why does any abused person go back? Familiarity is one reason; low self-esteem is another. Afterwards, I felt so remorseful, so I began changing my atmosphere. That only lasted for so long. I was playing with sin; I did not completely turn away from it. I'd repent and turn right back into the mess I repented from. I looked out my bedroom window one day and saw "Shorty" sleeping in his car, in the parking lot of my apartment complex. I felt bad for him as it was cold and he had burned all his bridges. I let him in as he promised to only take a shower and not disturb what God was doing in my life. He told me he was so proud of me and kept his word. However, when he began to make my life a living HELL, I knew it was spiritually wrong for us to be living together. If there's one thing I've learned from this, never keep your temptations close to you. You keep them far away ... far, far away.

One day I did or said something Shorty didn't like. He caught me in the hallway of our apartment and began to choke me. I attempted to pull his hair to get away from him, but he was too strong. I began to lose consciousness when suddenly his hands began to loosen around my neck, and then his hands grasped his chest. He said, "Call 911. I am having a heart attack." I told him, "The *^& I will! You do it yourself." I left the house for him to fend on his own.

And, no, that wasn't the end of it. I went back to him again and again and again, until God had to step in. Even though God had cleaned me up from drugs, the stronghold the devil had on me through Shorty was one only God could break! I wanted Him to break that stronghold and eventually He did. in the meantime, something was missing and that was giving God my heart and turning completely away from it (Shorty) and turning to God. I wasn't using drugs anymore, but that man was worse than any drug. I said that I would not go back to him, yet he was now in my house.

I wanted to save him. Now I know the Bible warns about that in Galatians 6:1; I was trying to save him, and he did not want to be saved. You can try to get a person back if they have found another lover, but you do not have a chance when that person has met the Lover of their Souls, Jesus Christ, and God was working on me.

I was lying on my bed one day. I lived upstairs and my bedroom window was next to an empty field. I did not have a television at that time, and no one was home with me. I am not sure what thoughts were running through my head, but I heard, "Darlene." It was a man's voice, but it was not harsh or scary. I gasped, jumped up off the bed and ran into the living room. No one was there. I checked the door; it was double bolted. I checked the bathroom. No one was there. I wasn't scared but I thought I was going crazy. As the years went by, studying the Bible, I realized who that was. Just like Samuel, God called my name. I felt a sense of purpose in me.

Soon after, I started going to Apollo College. Well, that's what it was back then. Now it's called Carrington College. Even though my ex and I were not having sex, we moved into a two-bedroom. He had his room and I had mine. We were not having sex, and I want to make that clear, as I had made up my heart as God dealt with me. One thing that I did not do and that I did not know as being a young believer was taking everything to God in prayer. I did not pray about this of course.

As I mentioned earlier, I wanted to help him. He went to the realty company and filled out an application to have his name on the lease. The realtor gave me a call and she asked me was I sure that I wanted this man to live with me. She asked, "Do you really know him" as she was looking at his background. I said, "Yes, I pretty much know everything." At this time, we had been together or knew each other for four years give or take a few years. So, as I started school, he accompanied me for support in taking my entrance exam. Now at that time, I did not have a High School Diploma or a GED, and I just knew I was not going to pass that test. Well, I made it and I started school as a Medical Assistant.

Things were going well. I would come home, and the house would be cleaned and dinner cooked. This impressed me, but really the times before we moved in and he slept at that house he would clean up for me and cook for the kids. Not long after he joined the school. We were together in some classes, but then he began to get high and come to school high. They saw it and I saw it. He was kicked out not because he was dozing in class but because he refused to do a drug test. Then he started leaving the house and coming back late or was away days at a time. I also remember someone telling me that we may not be sleeping together, but your good deeds are perceived as evil and you maybe leading someone to stumble (Romans 14:16). A lady I met at church who became my mentor gave me this advice. To this day, she has always been there for me, guiding me and supporting me in every way.

Well, my home life had gotten even worse. I remember on Thanksgiving Eve, he started drinking and doing spiteful things, like turning the oven off on the ham that was being cooked for Thanksgiving dinner. I couldn't tell him to leave because he was on the lease. What a big mistake I made. I was shacking up with the devil—entertaining an evil spirit. After waking the next morning and not smelling the ham, I looked in the oven and it was almost cold. I then saw that the oven was turned off. I was mad, but I had given up. I walked to the bedroom and put on some warm clothes. I picked up some money from the dresser. My plan was to walk to the Circle K on the corner, buy a fifth of Seagram's Gin, and call the old numbers to get someone to bring me some dope. I was done! Well, as I mentioned, that was my plan and not God's.

Our apartment complex had a long driveway. As I made my way down the stairs out into the parking lot, I got halfway and looked up and saw an older man coming out of a gate across the street from the apartment complex. I thought that was weird as it was cold outside and early in the morning, but he caught up to me as I made it to Blacklidge Street. I saw that he had a couple of bags in his hands, and that he was struggling trying to carry them as well as he had a long walking stick. God knew that I could not pass this man up, so I asked if he needed some help with his bags, hoping he would say no, but he said, "Why yes." As I took his bags, I began to walk faster. He was slowing me down and I wanted to get to the store. You see I had a plan! But the faster I walked, the slower he got. He even slowed down to take a rest as he leaned on his walking stick. As I looked back, I realized it was not a walking stick. It was long and taller than him; it was a staff. I asked where he was going. He said to the bus stop. I looked down into the bags he was carrying; it was a bunch of electrical cords. I asked him where he was coming from. He said, "My daughter's." I did not think to ask why he was not stay for Thanksgiving dinner as my mind was on drinking and drugging.

Anyway, we made it to Alvernon. The bus stop was right there on the corner. As we stepped up on the dirt, he began to tell me about a bike he had. I looked up in the sky as if to roll my eyes. He began to tell me it was a bike with baskets and a license plate. I replied, "Oh that's good." He said, "You know what that license plate said?" I hesitated but said, "No." He said, "Trust in Jesus." Right then I felt my heart dropped and I held back the tears. I sat his bags down on the bus stop. I wished him well and walked away and as I was walking away, he said "Remember. Trust in Jesus." Just then I began crying, sobbing and it started to mist. I turned around to see if he was there. He was gone. I wanted to thank him. Then I thought, "Gone! He could not have gotten too far. He walked slowly, and the bus had not come … and he was not across the street!" I knew that he was my Guardian Angel. I walked back home and began cooking again.

Over the next few weeks, things began to get even worse. I called my mentor a lot and she helped me with scriptures and prayers. She was a Godsend. The next day he and I almost got in a fight, but this fight was different. I was fighting back which shocked him. He was on the phone with the police and I had a table leg in my hand. I was ready to beat the h*** out of him. I knew he had to go, but what could I do? Nothing! I allowed the devil to sign the lease, and he signed on the dotted line. I called my mentor that evening and I shut my bedroom door. I still do not know to this day how he heard what we were talking about, but he did.

She suggested that I go downtown and get a restraining order on him and have them serve it. Guess what! He beat me down to the place. One day after I had arrived home from school, he was acting weirder than he usually did. I had finished my homework, washed the dishes and was getting ready to retire for the evening, when there was a knock on the door. As I walked out of my bedroom to get the door, his bedroom door shut. I answered the door and I was served. Shocked, hurt, crying and doubting God's promises over my life, I called Stoney and told her what happened. All she said was, "I'm coming over to see what is going on." She arrived and they had a talk and she told me I could stay with her until I could get a new place. Knowing this, I knew that my stay with her would be short as I wanted to not lose my freedom and security in housing. As I began throwing stuff out of my closet, crying and yelling at God, he had the nerve to come in my room and try to console me. One look into my eyes, he walked back out. I screamed, "You said you were never going to leave me! I thought you told me that you loved me! I thought you said you had a plan for me! Is this it God? What is going on?"

I was five months into school with four months to go before I graduated and I loved it. I was dedicated to finishing it. However, I had a problem. I needed a place to stay and did not know what to say to the leasing agent who had tried to warn me about Shorty. Stoney lived far away and there was only one bus to get there from her house. It would be a two-and-a-half-hour bus ride there and back, and the closest bus stop to her house was miles away. How was I going to get to the bus stop? I had to walk, that's how. I had to get up at three-ish in the morning to take a shower and to walk a mile and a half, 30 minutes to the bus stop, going and coming from school. It was dark and the Javelina'swere out. I was scared to say the least. I was also disgusted that she did not offer to take me to the bus stop. I said to myself, "Why did I agree to come live in her house?" I was hoping she had changed. However, never make decisions out of haste. One day I was leaving and Stoney's husband was leaving for work. I had gotten down the street a bit. It was pitch black and I was so scared. I prayed the whole way. He asked if I wanted a ride to the bus stop. What took me thirty minutes to do took him three minutes to drop me off.

He had done this for about a week or so until Stoney found out. It was not a big secret and I thought she told him to do it. I never expected him to take me, and nothing inappropriate ever happened. I got up as usual to leave and to my surprise Stoney was sitting up with him. I said, "Good morning." I saw the look of disgust on his face, and I knew then that she did not want him to take me any longer. They must have had a talk about him taking me because before as I left out of the door, she gave me a book light. A book light? What the *&^ for? "What is this going to do against a wild javelina?" I shot back as I walked out. I did try to use it and, of course, it did nothing. I attempted to shine the light on my hand, but it was not strong enough. I guess this was her way of making herself feel good. If she did not want him to take me, why didn't she give me a ride? You may say, "Well, she did let you live in her house." True, however with that type of help, who needs help at all? Why did she bother to let me live in her house when she was going to treat me like crap? Maybe she really wanted to help me out, but was conflicted on the inside with insecurities. Sometimes when people assist in helping you, they really don't know what type of help they want to extend to you.

LifeScript 8

SATAN KEEPS TRYING TO KILL ME

Nothing in this world could have stopped me from going to school. One day while riding the bus back to her house, I received a call from the lady at the realty company. She told me she heard what happened, asked me if I was alright and told me that she was going to investigate what she could do and get back to me in a few days. Well, by then I had been at my sister's house for almost three weeks. I received a call from Shorty telling me he was in the hospital and that he had a heart attack. I told him he was lying. He said, "No I'm not. Come down and see." He took something from me this time and I wanted it back. I didn't care about the heart attack or the fact that he was in the hospital; all I cared about was seeing him cuffed to the bed. The next thought on my mind was that I could get my place back and move out of my sister's home. I arrived at the hospital and sure enough he was in there handcuffed to the bed. I asked what happened. He told me he got caught selling pain pills to an undercover, and it felt like he was having a heart attack. I turned and walked out of the hospital. The next day I was standing in my old apartment. That sounds cold-blooded, but it serves him right to have me served with a restraining order when I kept him from sleeping in his car and put a roof over his head. You can't mess with God's children and get away with it. And there is no way evil can trump good.

He had the locks changed, but I was able to get in by using some skills that I had learned from the streets. The house was clean. I looked in the refrigerator and it was full of food and the freezer was full of meat. He had never bought that much stuff when he was living with me. I gave Stoney most of it as I began to gather things to throw in the trash. I did not want the cleaning company finding paraphilia, etc. I flushed it, threw out the tools that he was using to get high on and afterwards I called my landlord and told her what had happened. She had the same thought as me: you cannot do people wrong and get away with it for too long. She told me she had found a better place for me and that she knew I'd like it. I went there and I did. She has never charged me a move-in fee. This was another sign now that I look back that God had control of and was paving the way for me. When my ex had me served with a restraining order, I accused God of not loving me and taking care of me and not keeping His promises to me. It wasn't that God did not love me, but it was the choice I made to keep (Shorty) in my home and ignore what I knew was right and from that choice, resulted the consequences. The book of Proverbs talks about being under the same house with a contentious woman; in this case it was a man. God's hands were over me the whole time. Lesson learned.

I moved out of Stoney's house, and moved into my new apartment which by the way was less than fifteen minutes from the school. It was a month and a half before my internship when I noticed that the pain from my monthly cycle was getting unbearable. I went to the OB/GYN and she told me that I had fibroids that were causing the heavy flow. I was given the choice to remove the fibroids again or have a partial hysterectomy. Looking at the quality of my life when it was that time of the month and going without one ovary, it was a no-brainer as I was not having any more children. That was decided years ago. I took off from school, on medical leave, which meant I could come back on doctor's orders to finish the program and graduate. I went through the surgery just fine, and I was able to go back to school. I completed my internship and graduated in the early part of 2011 from Carrington College as a Medical Assistant. To this day, I do not know why God took me that way. To me, it was backwards because I still did not have my GED. But as the Word of God tells us, "My ways are not His ways." (Isaiah 55:8)

A year after graduation, the pain increased, and I had to go back in and have the other ovary removed. I was devastated as I thought this would take my womanhood away. I could not help thinking, "This is not fair. I did not ask for this!" From the last surgery, I learned that I did not prepare my home after the surgery correctly. The day before the surgery, I moved things down from the shelf and had set the water on the top shelf. Bathroom items were set up so that I did not have to bend or reach too high up. So, the day after the surgery, they suggest you get up and move around for a few reasons and one of them was so that you do not get blood clots. I attempted to get out of bed, and I felt something pop inside my stomach. I told the nurse and she came and looked at my bandages and they were not soiled so she figured that nothing was wrong. I bugged the nurse so much that she called in my doctor who pushed so hard on my stomach you'd thought someone was cutting me open alive. That's what it felt like. I screamed at the top of my lungs!

The one thing I remember that really ticked me off was they had given me a pain pump and put it in my hand. If you did not push it often, the pump would lock and the nurses had to come and unlock it. Well, they sure were mad at me. Did I care? No! I was newly in recovery and I was not going to get hooked on pain medications. They called my doctor in and she told me I had to take something. I agreed with her but told her it would not be a narcotic. She respected my wishes and gave me 800 mg of ibuprofen instead.

The next day I was released. I got home and was so happy I could rest and move forward. At that time, I was still at the little church, and the Pastor's wife came to check on me and tidied up a bit before she left. A few nights went by and the pictures on my wall began to move around.

My temperature hit 108 at times so off to the ER I went. They performed numerous sonograms and couldn't find anything and of course the fever was gone when I arrived there. Over a period of three weeks after my surgery, this kept happening: high fever and pictures and items moving on my wall.

On the next trip to the ER, I chose University Medical Center and that was the best choice I had ever made. By this time, I had lost 20 pounds within three weeks. I was not eating, and I needed help. UMC was a teaching hospital for students. When I arrived, one of the doctors looked at me and said, "Take her back STAT!" Off I went to the back. What we did not know was a massive hematoma was growing at a fast rate in my stomach. The reason they could not detect it was it was hidden behind my gallbladder. But as it proceeded to grow, they were able to detect it. When I arrived at UMC, it was the size of a soccer ball. As I look back, God kept me because He had a plan for me and not only that; He was teaching me how to trust Him. To trust Him through every trial, every circumstance, no matter what others say or don't say, what it looked like and how I felt, He was there. He was with me. He was quiet, but kept a close watch over His Child.

They admitted me bedside at the same time the nurses were hurriedly hooking me up to two bags of antibiotics and this was around the clock every hour. They wanted to keep an eye on it to see if the antibiotics were working or if they needed to do surgery. At that time, I did not know what type of surgery they would have to do. I had to keep my faith and know without a shadow of a doubt God sent me there. I called the Pastor's wife to let her know that I was back in the hospital and asked if she could please check my mail. She came down and gave me my mail and a scripture. She also prayed over me and told me that God said I shall not die but live and declare the works of the Lord (Psalm 118:17). I received that and did not know later that day I would need it. About noon my roommate arrived. There was a curtain that divided our beds, but I heard them wheeling her in and telling her it was her new room. The nurse spoke to her little bit about her care and what to expect next. I remember her asking the nurse when she would be able to take a bath. The reply was that the other nurse coming on will be able to help you with a sponge bath.

As I was lying in my hospital bed, I remembered my youngest daughter had called me a month ago with a dream she had that I was going to die. I quickly dispelled that memory, but when she called me in the hospital, I let it go to voicemail. She's my daughter and I love her, but I did not want to hear anymore of her crazy dreams. I was battling something bigger than me and I did not need to give any ammo to the devil. At that time, my children were in their teens and were with family members that were "supposed" to take care of them. I found out from my youngest as I was sharing my book with her that she was put out of my sister's (my sister's!) house and was taken in by her friend's mother. My youngest told me like she thought I knew. My heart began to sink and I got a sick feeling in my stomach as I thought to myself, "She was only fifteen at the time. Why would family do this to her? Who would do that to a child?" After I got over the initial shock, I told her, "I am not surprised. They treated me the same way." This recalls the story of Joseph in the Bible. In Genesis 50:20a, Joseph told his brothers, "You meant evil against me, but God meant it for good." My oldest daughter is an entrepreneur and she's working a full-time job. My son is working, taking care of his son. And my youngest has a double Bachelor's, one in Business and the other in Finance. She's currently working in Human Resources for a global company in New York. I am proud of all my children and I am so grateful to the Lord for watching over them.

Back to the hospital, the doctor and his team of students came in about 1 pm. The doctor told me that they were going to do another x-ray of my stomach to see how fast the hematoma was growing. He did not tell me that if it's still growing, they would have to do emergency surgery on that same day. I was not prepared, but God was; He's always watching over us. Stoney had stopped answering her phone for me or responding to text messages. I wanted to let her know that I was in the hospital. I am not sure why, although I guess I expected her to come, despite the way she treated me. Even today I am learning that the greatest upset of humans is expectations of others. Nevertheless, out of all the people, only one person besides my pastor's wife came to visit me. Believe it or not, it was my ex (Shorty)! I asked him how he found out I was in the hospital. He told me that he had seen the Pastor and he told me where you were. Oddly enough he was decent and he helped me. No matter what he may have done to me at times, there still is a loving person down on the inside. He helped me out of the bed to the restroom, to walk, and he combed my hair and he fed me when I couldn't do it on my own. He did not ask for money or anything. He came to see about me and helped me. No one else in my family did anything for me at that time, although my youngest eventually came to see about her mamma.

After he left, I went to sleep. They did not give me any pain medications at all. I would not have taken them anyway as I was not in any pain. When my fever went up, they gave me Tylenol. I was up early the next morning, sick and throwing up. When they were doing their rounds, he came and told me that they were going to prep me for surgery right away! I said, "I thought I had to be fasting." He said, "We do not have time for that. Despite the very strong antibiotics, the hematoma is growing rapidly." I waited for an hour and as I was waiting, I began to pray. Just then the nurse for my roommate came in and began to give her a sponge bath. I never saw my roommate's face and did not want to. As the nurse began to bathe her, she began to talk dirty to the nurse, telling her to wipe in certain places. The nurse told her, "I am not going to do that, and if you keep talking to me in that vulgar tone, I will leave you the things for your husband to do it." She kept on and the nurse gave her the stuff and told her to wait on her husband and she walked out.

As I waited for them to come and get me, my voice message prompt reminded me that I had not heard my daughter's message. I said to myself,

"I will listen when I got back from surgery." What I am about to tell you next is real. There are demons out there and Satan wants our faith and our souls. Just then my roommate asked me how I was doing. I paused for a minute and said, "I am fine." She said in her "normal voice," "Did they tell you?" I thought to myself, "What is she talking about?" I paused for at least a couple of minutes, and said, "Tell me what?" As she began to speak, her voice had changed into something deep and demonic as she replied, "That you are going to die." I looked up towards the top of the curtain that was separating us, thinking if anything comes flying over this curtain, it's on up in here. I was ready for a fight. As the saying goes, "If you stay ready, you don't have to get ready!" Armed with the Scripture my Pastor's wife gave me, I shouted that promise until my voice was hoarse. "I shall not die but live and declare the works of the Lord." I screamed, "Get out of her Satan! Get out! In the Name of Jesus, leave! You are a liar straight from the pits of hell!! Get out! I am a child of the Most High God!" Just then all her alarms were going off. The nurses ran in and said, "Get her out stat!" At that point, I did not care if she died or not. Just get her out! They moved her fast. The nurse asked me what happened, and I told her, and she was not shocked at all. She asked me if I needed to see a priest. I said, "Somebody! Ya'll got me twisted up in here!" She came back later—and I had calmed down—and told me that the priest would be in after my procedure. As they wheeled me out of the room, I was quiet on the inside. I did not know what they had in store for me. I didn't know if they were going to open me up. Just then I remembered what the nurse said. It was a "procedure," not surgery.

As I was being wheeled to the surgical room, I saw people sitting in the waiting area and one of them I noticed as my old landlady from the Section 8 Housing Department in South Tucson. I asked the orderly to stop. I said, "Hello." She asked me what was going on. I gave her the short of it and I asked her what was going on and she told me she was there for her husband. She wrote her number down and put it in my hands as she said a prayer for me, and she wrote down mine. As I arrived in the room, the first thing I noticed was the coldness of the room. There were no pictures on the wall, but there was music softly playing in the background. I desperately needed something to focus on. Just then God gave me another song to sing.

They wheeled me under this huge machine that was shaped like an upside-down rainbow. The focus was on the stomach, so they positioned me under it so that the machine could show them the view of my stomach from the inside. I was able to see it too, which was a trip! The gentleman was so nice; he saw that I was nervous, so he gave me some background about himself. "I've done these numerous amounts of times," he said. "I am going to take you step-by-step through this process so that you will know what I am doing every step of the way. First, I have positioned the camera/machine over the part/ area of your stomach that I need to focus on in order to insert this tube, this drainage tube, pardon me. If you don't mind me touching your stomach … I have to get this tube right here where you see this large black blurb on the screen. This is where the massive hematoma in your stomach has grown." He then showed me a picture of the size when I came in two days ago. It had grown to the size of a basketball.

He then shared that he was going to numb me from the stomach down to my waist. He went on to say that I would feel him on the inside as well as be able to see him inserting the tube. "You will be able to move your toes and wiggle your feet if you want. It will take the medication a few minutes to take effect. I will be over there preparing what I need to put on the tray. You can talk to me if you want. I am not far away. But I do want you to let me know if you feel pain and not the tugging of me on the inside." I agreed. He came back and sat down next to me. Apparently, he had stuck me with a pin, and I did not know it. But he told me after he did it to let me know that the shot he had given me had worked. This was not the first time I had this done. I was numbed when I had my tubes tied. I saw, felt and heard everything they were talking about.

Anyway, I could not take watching him any longer, so I began to sing "You don't know like I know what God has done for me." I sang and wiggled my feet back and forth. He was done. Whew! He then showed me a long tube hanging from my side. It was a drainage tube to drain the infection into a bag that needed to be measured on the hour to see how much was coming out as well as the color. I asked, "Will I be able to smell it?" He smiled and said, "No you will not, but this will remain in for three weeks."

I was then wheeled back to my room. My roommate was gone. I settled down in my bed and the nurse for that shift came in, greeted me and introduced herself. She then told me that the nurse on the shift before me told her what happened and that the priest would be in shortly. I was sitting up on the side of the bed when he knocked on the wall. I had to put another gown over my backside and I told him to come in. He greeted me and said, "You asked for a Priest?" I replied, "Yes, but that devil is gone now." He said, "Sister, I can tell you are a mighty woman of God, just by the way you said that. If you'd like or feel up to it, can you tell me what happened?" I agreed and after the story he told me; "That's the way you have to talk to the devil. You cannot play around with him because he isn't playing with you." You would not believe the things that I have seen as I walked these hospital corridors late at night. The devil feeds off souls in the hospital. You did right. Would you like for me to pray?" I agreed, and he wished me well after the prayer.

Two days later I was released. I was given a home nurse that would come to measure how much of the infectious blood was in the bag. She came only once and after that I was on my own. I was told not to lift anything, bend, etc. I had not prepared for that. I called my old landlord and she came over with no hesitation. I had purchased some frozen foods, and she began to prepare that for me. I thanked her and was so appreciative.

I told her that I needed a way to take a shower. She found a wire hanger in my house. That was a first … I can't stand wire hangers. They were a trigger to me as I used them to clean out my crack pipes. I thought I'd gotten rid of all of them so the fact that she found one was a God thing. She rigged it so that it could hang from the shower while I took a bath. It was a very sensitive area so I did not want it to come loose, but I saw it was taped down really well. So I took a shower and ate. Before I went to sleep, she told me she was going out of town and would not be able to help me further. She put everything next to me at counter height, especially my water, as of course I did not have time to prepare for this emergency surgery. A week went by and the case and a half of water ran low. I could not call my old landlady as she was not in town, nor did I feel I could I call my Pastor's wife as she had done enough for me.

I really hesitated to call Stoney. But I finally decided to and told her of my surgery. I do not remember what she said word for word, but I do remember what she said afterwards. Before I get into that, my mentor at that time had left Tucson and when she did my heart fell. I just knew that I was not going to make it and that our friendship would not be the same. But she had told me to stop expecting so much from Stoney. "She can only give you so much." So back to what I was saying, I asked her if she could come and pick up my food stamp card and go to the store for me and get water and something microwaveable. What she told me next floored me. I knew then that my mentor had told me the truth and after Stoney said this to me, I never expected anything else from her ever again nor did I ask anything else of her even to this day. Stoney said to me, "I can't come help you out. My dog just had surgery and I have to stay home and watch him." I hung up the phone. I could not say anything or think of anything but what she had just said to me for hours. You ever had that thought after the fact. Looking back now, I can see God wanted me to lean and depend on Him and wait for Him to send someone. To this day, that shocks me. I know that some people consider their dogs to be a part of their families, but this cuts the cake. I am speechless even now. So I prayed and God reminded me of the cab I caught a while back and the gentlemen gave me his card. I called him. He came right over and drove me to the grocery store, and I paid him to take my stuff upstairs and not only that he asked me where I wanted him to put things at. To the best of my recollection, I have never asked Stoney for anything else.

LifeScript 9

WHEN GOD HAS A PLAN...

A week later, I went back for a follow up to remove everything. I began walking with God much closer once I had a lot of time on my hands after graduation. God was leading me to get my GED. About the time I was moving again, I found a place called El Rio Neighborhood Center. I decided to sign up when I was settled in my new place. I began GED classes in 2012. It was hard and I thought I was too old, but God kept working with me—building my faith and strengthening me as I walked with Him. Month after month, I took the practice test and came up short. A good friend of mine asked me if I was trying to remember it or learn it. Wow, what a revelation! I was trying to remember it and not learn it.

As I left the store-front church, I felt the spirit leading me back to the church where Pastor Chris Dehan was pastoring. He asked me how I was doing, and I told him about how I was doing in math and asked if he knew anything about it. He offered to help tutor me and he did. This was in the daytime and with people there at the church and his office door was always open. He did not want anyone to get the wrong idea and neither did I. God used him in a mighty way. He showed me shortcuts and I knew that if I had a GED book so that I was able to study from home I'd be able to do more. I mustered up the courage to ask if the church could help me and they did. I found a used book for nine dollars and a seed was sown into my life and look where it has gotten me to this day. Never ever place a minimum amount on a gift God has planted into someone. We all know what we can do with a mustard seed, two mites and a few fish and loaves! (1 Corinthians 3:6-7, "I planted the seed, Apollos watered it, but God has been making it grow. It's not important who does the planting, or who does the watering. What's important is that God makes the seed grow.")

It took a year and a half to obtain my GED. It was hard to say that least. God had a plan and that GED was a small part of a big picture. There was a poetry contest for all who wrote a poem to be submitted to the Arizona Adult Literacy Week Completion. I submitted a poem and it went like this.

"Life"
What I see is people who remind me of how I used to be.
They are at the bus stops in the parking lots, I don't know their stories, and some say why do you care? Life's unfair for all, but to me they matter. I do care.

I was one of the students who was awarded the Distinguished Merit Award in 2013. I was so proud of myself and my faith was through the roof.

I decided after I achieved my GED, I would go thank Judge Wilson for what he'd done for me. If it was not for God using him, I would not be where I am today. I wanted to share what I had been doing, my success after I passed my GED and my graduation from Carrington College. I had begun my membership at Rising Star Baptist Church and had been there two years. It was the end of September and I had taken my share of practice tests for the GED so I had decided to do it! I had been meditating and praying and Pastor Chris Dehan had tutored me in math and I was sure it was time. After all, it was almost eighteen months since the journey started.

One of the prominent agencies in town paid for my GED testing. I could not afford to fail; therefore, I had no choice but to pass all of them. I prayed and meditated on Isaiah 26:3. On the day of the test, I was so nervous and the lady was late. I rocked back and forth in the hallway chair. I walked and quoted scriptures. I had my small pocket Bible and I quoted that scripture back and forth. As the testing began, I wanted to take all five tests, one at a time. Even though I came across some obstacles, God walked me through it. After I passed the first three tests, I was told she needed to leave, which left the writing of the essay and math to come back and take, but I was so full of faith at that time no one could have told me anything negative. No devil could stop me! I studied and went back the following Wednesday and passed! As I walked to the bus stop, I cried all the way. His words says in Hebrews 11:16, "But without faith it is impossible to please him: for he that cometh to God must believe that he is, and that he is a rewarder of them that diligently seek Him." Hallelujah!

I was so high in the Spirit of the Lord, it seemed like it took me a week to calm down. I was off to see the Judge as court was in session that day, I waited 'til that last person was seen. As he looked out into the courtroom, he asked me if he had missed my name on the docket. I replied, "No, my name is Darlene Gonzales and I stopped by today to thank you for sending me to the women's shelter." He looked over his glasses and smiled, shaking his head at the same time. He said, "Oh, my goodness." He came down from his bench as I began to show him what I've been doing and the church that I was now attending. He said to me, "Stay at Rising Star. Amos Lewis is a good man and a great pastor." I shared what happened at the women's shelter. I shared the volunteer work I was doing twice a year at Gospel Rescue Mission and how God has truly blessed me. We talked for what seemed to be hours. He told me his path as a child, what he did before he became a Judge. "What!" I said, "You owned a nightclub?" "Yes, and God called me to become a Judge." We laughed about the things he said I would do in court; however, I have never entered his courtroom with ashy feet. Hilarious! I do not believe that to this day.

He had a friend who was a Judge at that time who sat on his bench when he was not there. I did not like the spirit that was on him right from the get-go and he knew that. Let's call him (Scandalous). There's something on the inside of all of us that warns us about certain people, and he was one of them as my discernment proved true later. When the Spirit of God shows you something about someone, you'd better take heed.

Judge Wilson asked if I wanted to do volunteer work for him at the court, taking a census on the people's feedback of the court. I'd be working with an intern. I was so excited I said, "Yes of course." I volunteered for a month or so and I remember he encouraged me to put in an application at the courthouse, but I could not be cleared to work there. I did not know at that time he was retiring his bench. One day I received a call from one of the ladies that worked at the front desk. "Judge Wilson has papers for you to pick up at the window," she said. That call bugged me all night. What papers could he be giving me I asked myself. This young lady had an issue with me, and ladies you know what I mean. She would never look me in the face. She presented herself as better than me. I felt as if she talked down to me every time I had contact with her. But I kept believing and kept loving and showing respect, even if she did not show respect towards me. One day I handed her an application for employment. I could have sworn she almost passed out. Her eyes were a little glazed and almost twirling in her sockets. I rang the bell, and as she approached the window, I attempted to hand her the application. She looked at me and said, "Leave it there; I will get it later" and proceeded to walk away. Leave it where! I rang the bell again and she came back and I stuck it through the plexiglass.

After I picked up the papers from her, I walked back to the bus stop. I opened the white manila envelope. The shoplifting charge that carried a fine of $300.00 was the first one I pulled out. At the bottom of the page, it read "(Remove From Collections, Suspend Balance, and Close file)." And there were one or two more like this. God knew this would become a hindrance to me getting in the field He wanted me in, so he used Judge Wilson to make a way! I became teary eyed. It felt like a weight had been lifted off me. It didn't stop there. Judge Wilson had a colleague (another Judge) that worked in the City Court where my driver's license was suspended. Judge Wilson contacted him and off I went to City Court. My file was so old he walked it in from the archives. I was able to pay $25 monthly until the fine of $2,000 was paid off. However, later God even made a way for me to pay the full amount in a lump sum.

As I continued with my membership at Rising Star, I met a lot of people and to this day most of them still play a major role in what God is doing in my life. I met another Judge and his wife who would play a huge role in my life according to God's will and plan for me. I began seriously looking at all the ministries at Rising Star and said to the Lord, "What do you want me to do?" He led me to the Evangelism Ministry which was no surprise to me as I look back over my life. I met gentlemen there as he was the leader at that time of the Evangelism ministry. He spoke words of wisdom into my life, and encouraged me to become what God has called me to be. When someone sees the calling God has over your life and they're not jealous of it, it is a blessing. I remember one word that he kept drilling into me: "servanthood." Every time I had a complaint or an issue about doing anything, he would say "Servanthood Sister, Servanthood!" The team cleaned the wash across the street from the church, and the park as well as painted tables and an area outside of the church.

I had slowed down on the feeding ministry as God was moving me in a different direction. My season was up. I began, by the leading of the Holy Spirit, to evangelize at bus stops. Wherever I went, it did not matter, I was on fire for the Lord. (Romans 1:14 How, then, can they call on the one they have not believed in? And how can they believe in the one of whom they have not heard? And how can they hear without someone preaching to them?) I remember one time, walking to the bus stop on Oracle and Glen. I would always pray before I left and waited for God to speak, give me peace or a vision. As I waited, this one time God showed me the very bus stop I was going to, and the spirit came upon me. I cannot describe the feeling; it was almost like I was shielded with something. What I found out later is that God was preparing me to meet Satan or a few of his agents at the bus stop. Well, I walked up and everything around that bus stop was weird. There was a baby that kept crying and crying. I walked over to greet the mother and she looked at me funny as I looked inside the walker. The baby had weird colored eyes that I had never seen before. I handed her a booklet of the Gospel of St. John and she refused. I made my way around the bus stop as there were a lot of people waiting for the bus.

I went to the bus stop bench where three Caucasian men were sitting. They were laughing and talking, and they each had a can of beer in their hand. I greeted them and offered them either a Daily Bread or a Bible. They became infuriated. "What in the *&^ are we going to do with that? We don't believe in your God. If your God was real, why are there so many hungry people in the world starving?" No water and food and sick from disease, or helpless children?" I replied, "God has given all of us a way to help others, like employment, or some he has given wealth and He expects us to help others out with what He has graciously given us and by the way this is nothing new. If you've read the Bible, you'd know this happened back then and is still going on now. God's people have not changed. They are so inwardly focused, self-centered, they truly believe that what they have they achieved it on their own. You know the old saying 'I got mine – You get yours?' So, the poor become poorer and the rich become richer. What have you done with what God has given you?" They reached into their bags and showed me the remainder of the cans of beers. While this was all going on, this lady kept interrupting me, asking me if she could use my phone. First, I asked her to wait a minute, but she kept bugging me and I told her no. She said, "It's just like Christians to argue the word of God instead of helping out someone in need." I looked at her and said, "You have a gas station across the street. We are in front of an apartment complex. There is a Circle K on the other corner and plenty of people at this bus stop for you to ask. Get thee behind me, Satan!" She looked at me and walked away. She couldn't say anything else. She was exposed or that demon in her was. She had attempted to become a covert distraction, but not today. Anyway, so I turned around to continue my conversation and the gentlemen had become irritated at me and the Word of God, so they all stood up and simultaneously lifted their shirts. What I saw next was unbelievable. They all had 666 on their chests! I would say tattooed but this was not a tattoo. It was far from it. I have a tattoo and even when it was healing it did not look like this. They were born with it. The sixes resembled Old English numbers. The numbers were wide, and they were raised from the inside out. My God, My God!

Just then I did the best thing I could ever do, I bowed my head and I began to pray: "I proclaim that every knee shall bow, and every tongue shall confess that Jesus is Lord." I began to quote the Lord's Prayer and other scriptures. Just then the bus pulled up and they got on. The lady that wanted to use my phone was gone; the crying baby stopped crying; and the heaviness left that entire area around that bus stop. Say what you want, but I believe that the lady with the baby and the lady wanting to use my phone were protectors of those young men. I believe that the baby recognized my spirit and it bothered it as I approached, and they were all on assignment. Call me crazy, but you were not there, and you did not see the eyes that baby had. Satan is real and alive on planet earth; you'd better believe this as he has reign on earth until Jesus establishes a new heaven and a new earth. (Isaiah 65:17, Revelation 21:1). I fought with Satan on the streets, in the crack houses and in my family—he is real!

There was another time when I going to Walmart. I made it a rule to always take gospel tracts with me because you never know when the opportunity will arise to lead someone to Christ. The Oracle and Glenn area was part of the "Prostitution Track" back in the day and it still is now, but not so much as it used to be. Anyway, I was standing at the bus stop near Glenn on Oracle Road. I was dressed decent of course. As a car pulled out of the AM/PM, I stood some distance from the bus stop, as the patrons were smoking cigarettes. A car pulled up next to me and I noticed that it did not take off into traffic. The gentleman rolled down his window attempting to say something to me. I walked over to the car but not too close. He said to me, "How much?" I said, "How much?" He said, "Yes, how much?" I said, "It's free!" The look on his face was priceless. He said, "What!" I said, "It's free! All the Lord wants is your soul. He wants you to be free of sexual strongholds." I reached into his passenger side window and handed him a gospel tract.

It must have been a sign from God that he was not supposed to be out there as he looked up at me, eyes bigger than a deer caught in headlights, and spun off into traffic. I don't think he even looked for oncoming traffic. He sped off as if something was chasing him. That will fix him. Hilarious!

A year or so later, I received a letter and bill from the Fines, Fees and Restitution Enforcement (FARE) program. I did not think the mail was for me because my name was misspelled on the front of the envelope. However, the address was correct and as I began to read it, the statement said that I owed $450.00 and it was going to be collected or a warrant issued for my arrest. I proceeded to call the City of South Tucson's court and guess who answered, Ms. Prittzy! I greeted her and mentioned the letter from the FARE program and how they were attempting to charge me for something that the Judge asked her or whoever to strike from the record. She told me, "I can't do anything about that." I replied, "I did not ask you what *you* can do; I asked what this office can do about this. You were there,. You handed me the papers from Judge Wilson, and I know you read them as you were putting them in the envelope." She said, "You will have to pay it; that's all I have to say." I replied, "Why should I pay for your mistake?" She said, "If there is nothing else, I am going to end this call," and she did. She hung up the phone! That *** hung the phone up on me. So, I went down there. She could not look me in my face and tell me she did not have anything to do with the misspelling of my name. Yes, I accused her because she was the type of woman that would do some dirty stuff like that. Anyway, if that partition was not between us, I would have snatched her by that crooked sew-in she was sporting and stomped her with my so-called ashy feet. But I knew that would be wrong. There is always more than one way to beat a witch, so I attempted to reach out to (Scandalous) and asked him to get in touch with Judge Wilson about what had happened. He told me, "I can't do that. This is against the law for you to even reach out to me and ask me anything like this." What the *7%! You big headed *^%$! Here you are blessed by God to be able to help your brothers and sisters out and you do some (Scandalous) stuff like this. I was not asking him to pay the fine. I was not asking him to get rid of it because this was supposed to have been done in the first place. So, the very next week, I called the court again with a pleasant voice. The same girl answered and told me that (Scandalous) said we should not talk with you on this matter again. I said okay, smart #@*! If someone in that office did not know anything about this, how is it that the forms Judge Wilson gave you to give to me had the correct spelling and the statement from the FARE program doesn't? She said, "I am not sure." "Okay, so I am going to play dumb like you. This office must report unpaid fines, correct? I believe I heard something about that. So how is it that you are not being honest with me and leading me to who I have to speak to?" She said, "I am going to end the call now." So, I thought to myself, okay, maybe she doesn't know. But I still didn't trust her or (Scandalous.)

I was lost at that moment on what to do. Just then God led me to speak to Judge Anderson and his wife. At that time she lived down the street from me and had been a huge help to me when I was not working. She is such a sweet beautiful lady! They're pillars in the community. So, I told her about what was going on, and she led me to speak to her husband who at that time had retired from the bench as well. He told me that they cannot expect you to pay when it was a clerical error. He told me exactly what to do. "Write a letter addressing the newly appointed Judge and when you are done, call me and I will tell you the next step." When I finished the letter and read it to him, he told me to print a copy of the misspelled statement with my name on it and include the forms Judge Wilson gave you that said "fine paid in full, strike it from collections and send it to the current Judge."

Shortly afterwards, I received a letter citing a clerical error from the

FARE program stating that I did not have to pay the fine. Why couldn't Scandalous do this? Why couldn't he put aside whatever weight that was besetting him? Why couldn't he take off those rose-colored glasses and help me? Maybe God did not want my help coming from him. Not everyone who can help you is meant to help you. God knows the heart of man. He sees what we can't see. My life moved on by the grace of God whether they helped me or not.

Shortly after, I felt a tugging in my Spirit; I did not know what it was, but it would not leave me alone. God was leading me to become part of His family. His plan for my life was becoming a licensed Minister. I didn't know what that was, so I had a meeting with Pastor Amos Lewis, the Senior Pastor of Rising Star Baptist Church. He explained what I was feeling. He understood and said most people call it a notion or a knowing. I told him what I had been doing before I met him and became a member of Rising Star. I told him that my heart was passionate for the lost and homeless. He said, "If this is true, we have no formal training here for this, but if you feel God is calling you to do this, follow one of our ministers here that will show you how and what to do as she is so involved in the church and the community."

I asked that person and to say the least, she told me "I don't want anyone following me and bothering me. I don't do that." Well, I went back to Pastor Lewis and told him what she told me. He then said, "If you are serious about helping the homeless and helpless, I suggest you follow Pastora Diana."

LifeScript 10

DISCOVERING SERVANTHOOD

I called Pastora Diana and told her what Pastor Lewis wanted me to do. She accepted me and shared with me that she wanted me to come out to "Church on the Street" to see what it was like. One day I caught the bus out there. I did not know what to expect. I introduced myself to her and she gave me a hug and showed me around. She showed me the Men's House as well as the Women's House. The Women's House is the house the food for the homeless was prepared, cooked and served in. I thought when I went out; I was going to begin preaching, which I knew nothing about. She told me at that time that when you come out you do not start preaching first, but you serve first. The first word that came to my mind was ***servanthood***.

So, serving, and greeting people was what I did. If they needed help in the kitchen, that's where I was. The set up they had was amazing and it was almost like a church service. They heard the word first, and then they were served food, coffee and water. Sometimes there would be enough for seconds and at other times there wasn't. When Pastora Diana found out that I was taking the bus, it touched her heart. She began to orchestrate rides for me to get there. That's when I met the Preacher who was head of the Church on the Street and his lovely wife. She began to pick me up as busy as she was and not only for the Church on the Street feedings, for their park ministry and the nursing home ministry. We became best friends. What a powerful, humble, anointed woman of God!

I am not sure when I was asked to bring the Word, but I was prepared to share my testimony as God saw fit to help me with a fifteen-minute sermonette. That was about all that I could handle at that time. One day an Elder from Rising Star joined us. We tag-teamed and did an amazing job of sharing God's word and love. I found out about a ministry Pastora Diana was involved in called NANA Ministries in Tucson for families in Mexico. She shared with me the things that they needed. The pictures she shared with me moved and touched my heart deeply. The lack there while we had plenty drove me on a mission to call on favors from people in the community and in my neighborhood. More importantly, this move of God on my life would lead me to learning to witness and pray for the people in the parks as well as the nursing homes. God was laying a foundation— preparing me for what I am doing today—all because Pastora Diana opened her heart to mentor me and lead me in the way of the Lord.

I established Biblical relationships with a few of the managers at stores in my neighborhood. Safeway would allow us to set up donation tables. ACE Hardware would donate rakes. Home Depot donated the seeds the families needed to plant food. I remember a time when the Pastor's wife of Church on the Street and I drove around asking for food for Mexico. That day we collected 67 pounds of food from Walmart. Pastora Diana was headed on a five-day trip to Nogales, Mexico and she needed that food and God provided. At times making calls to different stores became arduous. I really had to stay motivated and know that God's will is for us care for the widows and orphans (James 1:27).

When visiting Santa Rosa Nursing facility, we would sing, Pastora Diana would play the guitar, which by the way she played beautifully, and we would sing songs that touched the hearts of those that were there. After singing, a message was brought and then we would go and pray for each person that raised their hands for prayer. After loading the cars, we would go to De Anza Park to evangelize and feed the homeless.

It seemed as if I was always on the go, asking for donations and collecting them. I would carry them on the bus if I could, or if it was too large Pastora Diana or someone from the ministry would pick them up. I remember the YWCA was giving away jackets, but when I arrived they were out of my size, so I got two jackets for a couple of teenaged girls in Mexico. Pastora Diana would call me after she arrived from one of her trips to Mexico and gave me a list of items to start working on for her next trip. God would do what He has always done; He exceeded our expectations.

One day after leaving the nursing home, we arrived at the park and began walking around speaking to whoever would listen to the Word of God. We were not just walking into a park but into their homes. There would be times people would sell drugs in front of us. They would smoke weed and curse. At other times, they would put it away until we left. That day I met a couple of ladies. Their names were Delores and Gigi. Any time, and even now in my ministry, I am careful where I step or even attempt to sit down at. Drug addicts will stash syringes, crack pipes, etc. at the park benches and even in the sand from others and especially from the police. I started talking to Delores., but I looked at Gigi and noticed bruises on her arms, swollen lips and bruised eye. Delores was a struggling addict and she admitted that the drug programs weren't helping her. "They're unable to relate to the struggles; therefore, they are not able to reach me nor understand what I was going through. They don't know what it is to be addicted to anything, so therefore their educations make them stupid. How can they even relate to me? I don't need some clinical definition. I need someone who has been where I have been to understand the struggle and who made it out." Gigi, on the other hand, was quiet. Compassion fell upon me for her, as the recollection of the brutal beatings of my past ran across my mind.

As her tears were streaming, I thought to myself, "I wonder if she is thinking, what did I do or say this time for him to hit me? What can I do next time so that he will not hit me?" These very same thoughts ran through my mind over and over for years in my past abusive relationship.

Gigi touched my heart deeply. I didn't want to leave her until she "Got It." As I was speaking to her about the love of Christ, she did not want to hear it and I respected her request. I must remember that someone plants, another waters and God supplies the increase. Gigi mumbled about four words the twenty or so minutes that I spent with her. She asked for prayer for her son to get off drugs. As I began to speak to her about my past abusive relations, I can tell what I was saying was registering to her by the tears that were slowly streaming down her face. We attempted to pray for Gigi. I sat on the opposite side of her as we attempted to create a circle around her in order to stand in the gap. She refused prayer for herself, as I did for years.

As time went by, I found myself going to the hospital to visit people, I was at the Pima County Jail singing Christmas Carols in the winter. The more I worked with Pastora Diana; I was able to see the love of God poured out in my life in a mighty way. After seeing a commercial about lost money, I was led by God one day to go to the IRS website for lost or stolen property. I just followed His lead and came to find out I had money that was left in a bank account I had closed at Chase Bank in 2008. I took everything out but the twenty-five dollars it took to keep it open. I had totally forgotten that I had the money left in that account. Anyway, I went to the website to retrieve it and I could not believe it. Two thousand dollars and some change had collected in interest all those years. We have blessings with our names on it. God knows how and when He will choose to disburse it.

Well, that was a blessing, but my driver's license was suspended, and I was still paying on it. Until I had it paid off, I cleaned houses and saved money; however, one night I added up the years it would take me at the pace I was going to pay off the fine for getting my driver's license back was three years. I said to the Lord, "It's going to take me too long to get it back." I don't even think that was a prayer. I was stating something He already knew. Well, that was on Saturday night. Sunday morning was church and as the church van approached my place, I greeted everyone and off we went. It was my Sunday to greet, and as I was standing by the opening of the doors of the Sanctuary, I heard someone say, "I don't see her. She isn't here. Darlene! Darlene!" An older lady walked up and said, "Girl. I was arguing with the Lord about you. I told him that I would not be able to find you in this big church." She said with urgency, "The Lord spoke to me last night and He told me to help you with something." I looked up at her with tears in my eyes and walked away heading to the lady's room waving my hands in the air and shaking my head. I couldn't believe it.

She said, "What's wrong? I have to do this now and I need you to pay attention to my instructions." She said, "Is there a bill or something you have to pay? I started giggling almost uncontrollably as she went on to say, "I don't care what it is; I know God told me last night to help you until the bill is paid off. Even when I go out of town which seems to be every month, you will get a check and when it's paid off you tell me." I couldn't believe it; I just could not believe it! I was floored to say the least. What would have taken me three years to pay off took only a year to pay off. She sent me money when she was back east and apparently she did do that a lot (going out of town I mean). She kept her promise to the Lord, and He kept His promise to me to take care of me and give me the desires of my heart.

As for the money from the IRS, I gave ten percent to my church and began looking on Craigslist. I purchased a car and my driver's license came the next day. Having a car made it so easy for me to get around and meet Pastora Diana in the community as well as pick up items in my car rather than on the bus. God is so good; sometimes it just takes a while for things to come around to you. All is needed is faith and obedience.

Pastora Diana asked me one day if I had identification and if I wanted to go to Nogales with her on her next trip. I said "Yes," with a little hesitation in my voice. She told me what time we would leave for the trip and she would call me in enough time so that I could be ready. She eventually called me, and our day started at 3:30 am, preparing to leave at 5:30 am. I didn't know what to expect. I've heard a lot of things about the border, but I wanted to keep my focus on doing God's work and know that He would keep us safe.

We arrived in Nogales, Arizona around 7:30 am. The trip up there was so beautiful. We crossed the border checkpoint safely and we stopped to change in some money for their currency. We dropped off food at the Church on the Street Discipleship Home in Nogales. We began opening boxes and bagging them according to where we were going. For example, we took a bag of protein bars into the prison, where they were evenly distributed. The dry milk and oatmeal would be given to the families that lived in the Dump, and the abandoned monastery for the orphaned children.

I was shocked, scared and excited at the same time as we drove in the city. You see things like this on television, but obviously it's a huge difference when you are there. Pastora Diana shared that when we crossed, we drove across a weighted scale and if they had detected the amount of food we had they might have charged us for it or turned us back around. Somehow they thought we would only be bringing that much food across to make money by selling it to the people, rather than just giving it to them.

As we drove down some of the narrowest, busiest streets I have seen in my life, I saw children standing in the middle of the street selling gum and adults selling some beautiful birds, fruit and newspapers as well as cleaning windows. I was told the people in Nogales, Mexico were only allowed to make one dollar a day, ten dollars max. I am not sure if this is true, but if it is it's horrible.

The police were all dressed in black with only a view of their eyes. Pastora Diana told me to never make eye contact as they were holding machine guns. I was thinking to myself, "What in the world? This is only hours from Tucson." It was unbelievable!

We arrived at a place called the Dump, and that's exactly what it is. The higher up the mountain you live, the poorer you are. It's backwards to us, as we see the people who live at the top of mountains as rich and the people down the mountain are poor. As we drove up a rocky, steep slope—which is a street to them—you get a first glimpse of the extreme poverty they live in and their daily lives. I saw children and the elderly digging things out of the dump: things to eat, things to wear, etc.

We finally arrived at the top of the mountain at a place called NANA. It's a small community center and church. Because of the multitude of children, their schools were on two schedules. The kids who could not read nor write nor had birth certificates were not allowed to go to school, so they would come and eat at NANA's house. The seniors as well as the widows also made their way up the steep mountainside on foot. They came for worship, prayer and to take home what was left after the children ate. What I noticed when I entered NANA'S house is they had cardboard for a roof and dirt floors. But they were grateful. They loved Pastora Diana and the people who came with her. Even though I did not speak their language, they loved me anyway. Love is a universal language.

For our next stop, we made our way back down the mountain to the Juvenile Detention Center, a thirty-minute drive. Upon arriving, there were two guards on the outside with machine guns standing behind a boarded wooden area and wired fence. They raised the arm and we drove through. In the vehicle, we gathered out IDs. After going through the formalities of checking in, we walked through a security door and stepped right into the living quarters of the prisoners. That was a shock!

Arms reached through the bars and everyone was yelling in Spanish. The first thing I noticed was the smell of mold. The quarters were not up to the standards of those in Arizona, of course. I thought about the time that I was jailed in Tent City complaining about sleeping outside in tents. Even in Tent City, it was not this bad. Americans have it good in every aspect, from life to eating, housing and prisons. They reached out and shook our hands.

There were five cells. Four out of the five cells housed five to six young men in each cell, ages varying from 13-17. And the other cell was for young girls, ages 11-17. This was shocking and detestable for me to see a young girl housed with the men in the same room but a different cell. I asked Pastora Diana what she could have done to be put in here. She replied, "She probably stole an apple … something to eat." I spoke briefly on Luke 15:4 as Pastora Diana translated the message and afterwards a young man gave his life to Christ. As we all were singing and praising God, we handed out the protein bars to them and to the guards on our way out. A few young men asked for prayer before we left. What an awesome experience for me to see this in this atmosphere. After leaving the prison, we drove ninety minutes to Hermosillo to get to Imuris where the Abandoned Orphanage was that housed fifty orphaned children. That was the place I really wanted to visit.

LifeScript II

NEVER GIVE UP ON NEW BEGINNINGS

We had finally arrived at the place I was most anxious to see. As we unloaded the food and items from the car, the children were screaming Pastora! Pastora! They were so happy to see her and it touched my heart. Diana then showed me where the children were staying. It was awful. There was neither reasoning nor justification to what I saw, and yet they seemed to be content with their living situations. They were all alone, with no parents to care for them, comb their hair, sing to them, or put them in bed. They had no security at all.

Later that day, we drove back to Tucson. I felt so guilty for the things that I personally took advantage of like clean water, a bed to sleep in, bathing soap, edible food and my grandchildren and how much I spoil them. I had safety, freedom of speech, laws that protect me, shelter, parks and so much more. I was so uneasy for a few days. While I was sitting one day, there was a Scripture in 2 Kings 7:3-4 that came to my mind. In short, those leprous men concluded they had nothing to lose by going to into the camp where they knew food and rest was waiting. I see now why there is a desperate need to cross the border. I know that it's right to do things the right way, but you've probably never lived in that manner.

I did another trip with Pastora Diana to Mexico. This was an overnight trip which I was uneasy about as I knew the degree of my OCD would kick in. As we crossed the border, we drove straight through Hermosillo. The

Mexican Police had up blockades on both sides of the highway. We went through three of them, and to this day I do not know what had happened, but it seemed to be the norm for living there. I had remembered what Pastora Diana told me the last time, not to look at them. As we drove nearer to them, they resembled ninjas. I saw their machine guns strapped to the top of their trucks. They were heavily armed. This was the type of stuff that I saw in movies or third world countries, not down the street so to speak from my home. Nevertheless, we had to drive through. We could not stop, nor could we turn around. As we approached the first blockade, we drove slowly. Something happened in the vehicle. Pastora Diana put some music on low and started praying and all I could do was just let the tears stream down my face. It was terrifying! Now I know what David in Psalm 27:5 meant, "For in the day of trouble, he will keep me safe in his dwelling; he will hide me in the shelter of his sacred tent and set me high upon a rock." Something rested down on me. I could feel it as it seemed to me that we were driving through some type of tunnel as everything even the music had faded. God was truly with us in the vehicle. We both were quiet for a while after we drove through that. Later, when we arrived back in Tucson, I asked Pastora about it and she simply said it was God's Sovereignty.

During our drive down long strips of the highway, I was taken back by God's magnificent handiwork. The mountains took my breath away. I noticed a large group of people walking; it was a pilgrimage. The people would walk for miles trying to get to a shrine called "Pagan God." If they had arrived on time and the shrine had fallen, then whatever they prayed for or hoped for wouldn't happen. They would put their hopes on this shrine to be standing when they got there. Wow! There were little makeshift churches by the roadsides to feed people, tend to their wounds or provide sanctuary. For those the statue had fallen on, they would have to set up the little makeshift churches as punishment. We drove ninety more minutes and finally we arrived in Imuris. There was a volunteer already there assisting with cooking spaghetti and refried beans. Lunch is at 2 pm and I got there in time to serve and clean up.

Pastora asked me to do the dishes and to me this was the wall that I did not ever want to hit: dealing with my OCD. There was no dish soap, hot water or gloves. I had to keep my mindset Biblical with prayers of gratitude and thanksgiving. There were bugs, huge spiders, and huge grasshoppers all around me. I tried not to think of every germ and disease that I would catch if I had a scratch on my hand or I would have walked out. The dish rag was so nasty, and it smelled gross. I did everything to keep a smile on my face and to keep from gagging. I needed the people to see me handling this like a champ; I did not want to hurt their feelings. After the dishes, I wiped down all the tables and chairs and swept the best that I could.

I walked back to the first building and sat outside looking around at the buzzards flying in the air wondering what had died, God provided me with peace. I was shaking on the inside and I wanted to regurgitate and take a long shower, and I was still a new Christian, but after that experience I felt I had grown years in my walk with Christ. I had gotten so comfortable saying; "I'm blessed" but coming there truly put meaning to those words. I like so many other Christians never know what we would do if He humbled us and allowed us to live in this manner. Would we still praise Him? Would our complaints be few? Would our worship be heartfelt? There are things that are so normal for us to have that we feel we "cannot" do without. Those things are scarce there and priceless.

Before dinner, Pastora Diana asked me to straighten out the closet with all the canned goods. There were mice droppings, roach feces and spiders everywhere. Diana told me the women did not know how to cook from a can. They were used to getting their vegetables from the ground. So, as we started preparing for dinner, we opened 30 cans of vegetables soup with a can opener that was rusty, and it seemed to have been used for other things, but we made it work. We also added numerous cans of beans to it. The dinner bell rang, and we served 50 children plus 2 adults. Even though we didn't think it'd be enough, God multiplied what we had.

There was no real supervision, home structure, hot water, sanitation, air conditioning or swamp cooling in the children's quarters, if you can call it that. I was told that families were basically forced to leave their children because of the economy. The oldest girl was 17 and she had been there since the age of 8 years old. She tried to disciple the younger children but to no avail, The severe poverty and filth that they were forced to live in was unbelievable. To be there and try to help was overwhelming to me. I went there thinking I was going to show them I know how it is to go without. Boy was I humbled. The people there really ministered to me, with humility, happiness, contentment, and no complaints at all (or at least I did not hear any). In many, many situations whether they had plenty or nothing at all, they were content. Being totally without, they still had the willingness to praise God, and to sing songs of praises to Him.

As we traveled back to the Dump as I mentioned before, it was on top of a mountain, they were having praise and worship and a wedding. I looked around at where I was, on top of a filthy trash heap. The houses had no floors and a plastic tarp for a roof. Sheep and goats were being herded in the background and people walked miles from the bottom of the mountain to come and praise God together. It was so unbelievable! A verse of a song they sang was translated to me and it went like this; "Because you even look upon us, we are so grateful. You have not forgotten about us like everyone else and we honor You for this." They showed such a reverence and honor for God that I have not seen since then. I did not have this much reverence for God, and He had brought me from a life of homelessness and drugs. I was humbled to say the least and it caused me to look inward and examine what I was praising and who I was praising. Could I praise you God, if you took all that you've given me away? This struck me to the core.

If it wasn't for the charity that was shown through just a few people, I believe that most of the kids wouldn't make it to see the age of 25. If you're feeling led to give, please check out the website for NANA ministry. We left headed back to Tucson; I was filled spiritually and tired physically.

The next few days I was getting concerned because I still felt drained. I called my doctor and a couple of weeks later I was diagnosed with fibromyalgia. I could not believe it ... It really was one thing after another. But as I began to stand on God's word for healing, and I still do, the pain left. The other symptoms are somewhat still present, but I just thank Him that He does not allow me to feel the full effect of this disorder. I spoke to Pastora Diana about stopping my trips to Mexico and she understood.

My focus went back inside the church and I was so surprised at the amount of static I received from women in leadership roles inside of the church. Even though Pastor Amos Lewis prayed over me, I still wanted to make sure that I was called to be up front, in the spotlight so to speak. I was told by some of the leaders in the church to sit down, "You just want to be seen." I was told that I was a crackhead and that I did not belong up there at the altar praying for anyone. I was so hurt to say the least and I did not ever want to go back in there. But let me say this, if you ever experience "church hurt" and you know that you have a calling upon your life and you know that God called you, don't ever allow the envy and wickedness of anyone else stop you from fulfilling that call upon your life. Amen!

I argued with God and He told me, "You are not leaving until I tell you to! Now go back and stand your ground." I went back Sunday after Sunday and it seemed to get better over time. I was looked over and still am to this day by certain cliques or I should say the haves. But that's alright! I was always a leader and never a follower. You will never, ever see me follow anyone who seems to think they're better than anyone else.

One of the sisters in the church befriended me. She told me to be careful of the "green-eyed monsters." She gave me the following Scripture and I stand on it today. It has brought me a long way and has taught me to stand my ground in the Lord, not only in the church but in the secular world as well. (Psalms 119:165 "Great peace has those who love your law, and nothing can make them stumble.") Pray this over all your battles. My friend has been instrumental to me in my walk with Christ. She is very knowledgeable in the Word and very down to earth. She has become more than my Sister-in-Christ; I can truly say that she is a friend of mine.

I decided to get a job in the field that God was calling me to and that's behavioral health. I received my first job and stayed there for three years.

I was having car issues and met with my Pastor in his office and he asked me about my time with Pastora Diana as we spoke more about my calling inside the church. He shared that the Minister's Conference was waiting for you to come in and join us. What he did not know is that I was wrestling with God as He was trying to remove the old me. My fight was against some of the nasty wicked spirits inside the Minister's Conference, but God wanted to do the fighting for me.

I stayed. I was so used to running away from my issues or fighting in my own strength out in the world. This is something that I had to allow God to do: let go and let God as they say. Trusting God was hard in the beginning. Let me tell you why. In the streets you trusted no one. Every day I needed to make enough money panhandling to get a room for one or two nights, and if I did not make enough money for a room, I'd pay a crack house to let me sleep in the corner on the floor, just so that I was safe. My food I had to get. My housing I had to get. My protection was in my own hands. No one was going to help me and if they did, they wanted half. I could have made it very nicely on the streets, if I had prostituted myself out. But that was not going to happen. I'd rob, beg, borrow or steal in order not to turn to prostitution. So, for me to suddenly trust someone (God), that I could not see was like picking a certain time of day and stepping out into traffic blindfolded. It was hard, but He kept me from fighting and cussing people out in the church. I was a hot mess and He was the purifier. On the other hand, the most astonishing miracles of life is living through something you thought would kill you.

So, as He began to show me that He was on my side even though I did not see Him or feel His presence at times, He was with me. I learned so much under our Senior Pastor Lewis. He is a true leader's leader and a minister's mentor; he understands and is patient. He teaches and guides us and gives us lots of books and articles, so we need to grow in the Lord. I would not be the Minister I am today if it had not been for his preaching, teaching, and guidance. He's given to all his ministers who sit under him.

As I began to grow, God had begun to speak to me through His word and through other people. I was licensed as a Minister in 2015. I went back to school and received my AAS at Wayland Baptist University in 2018. I was given a vision for a ministry in 2012, and it came to pass in 2013 and is still thriving to this day.

This feeding ministry was established by God and Him only. Therefore, from my past traumas, others can live and be set free as well. To this day we have fed close to four thousand people, led hundreds to Christ, clothed them, loved on them and shared God's word with them. You see trauma comes in all different types of colors, shapes, situations and backgrounds. If you can understand God's love, what it looks like, you can help anyone with trauma. Love covers a multitude of sins (1 Peter 4:8,) which simply means; intense love; for love shall cover a multitude of sins. If God has shown you love and forgiven all that you've done, we are commanded to love one another as we do ourselves. When I came to God, I had a truckload of sins to dump on Him,. much like the prodigal son, He did not tell me to get clean and come back. No, He welcomed me with open arms and so He will do the same thing for you.

Lord God, You have caused my heart, soul and mind to be so overtaken by your grace that I too share the testimony of the sinful woman who anointed Your feet in Luke 7:47-48 AMP. (Therefore, I say to you, her sins, which are many, are forgiven, for she loved much; but he who is forgiven little, loves little." [48] Then He said to her, "Your sins are forgiven.")

Heavenly Father, the gift that comes from my tears and behavior shows that my old life has ended, and a new life has begun. Your word "forgiveness" lifted my burden of guilt and the heaviness of darkness as well as shame. I responded with overflowing, heartfelt gratitude. I want to say thank you for giving me this love story, your story, for me to share. Amen.

If this book and God's Words have caused you to think about what you are doing, if it has given you any hope at all that you too can have a loving, lasting relationship with your Lord and Savior Jesus Christ, and you feel like you want to turn away from what you are doing, turning from your sin to Christ, asking Him to change your life and take total control of it, read on. And if you desire a shifting in your life right now, please allow this prayer to overflow in your heart.

Lord Jesus, I know that I have sinned against you and deserve Your punishment. I believe that You died on the Cross to pay for my sins. I choose now to turn away from my sins and ask for Your forgiveness. Jesus, I'm making You the Lord and Leader of my life. Change me! Help me to think right! Help me to walk right and talk right! Help me now to live the rest of my life for You and You only! Thank You for giving me life everlasting with You. Amen.

If you have prayed this prayer, please find a church that teaches the resurrection of Christ, that teaches Jesus is your Lord and Savior. I want to close with this. When God called me, he spoke to me gently and he dealt with me gently. Many times, He and I have had long conversations and at times it was just me sharing my heart to one of the best friends a single woman can have. He has ingrained it in my heart to trust Him in all my ways. Therefore, if you are a new Believer in Christ, Backslider or Seasoned Saint, trusting God with all our heart and mind is essential to your walk. Much like having water to drink in the desert, so is faith needed to walk with God.

Trust in God and He will show you great and mighty things. I have two things I want to give to you at the close of this, my very candid, transparent and true "LifeScript," Basically, I didn't give up! And I beg you, **"DON'T GIVE UP2" From Sunset to Sunrise** is my story of how I made the decision to allow the SON, Jesus Christ, to rise in my life.—the life-enriching decision to "live, move and have my being in Him" (Acts 17:28). And you can do the same.

To start this process, please use the LifeScript Journal pages to record your responses to what you got from my story and how it impacts your story. Your LifeScript is just as important to God as mine was and still is. Additionally, I want to leave you with a few Scriptures that have brought me thus far and will keep me forever.

MY FAVORITE SCRIPTURES

These are my favorites and I pray that they become yours:

I have been crucified with Christ; it is no longer I who live, but Christ lives in me; and the life which I now live in the flesh I live by faith in the Son of God, who loved me and gave Himself for me. Galatians 2:20 NKJV.

And we know [with great confidence] that God [who is deeply concerned about us] causes all things to work together [as a plan] for good for those who love God, to those who are called according to His plan and purpose. Romans 8:28 Amplified Bible

Delight yourself in the LORD, AND He will give you the desires of your heart. Psalms 37:3-4 NKJV

Fear not, for I am with you; be not dismayed, for I am your God. I will strengthen you, Yes, I will help you, I will uphold you with My righteous right hand. Isaiah 41:10

I will greatly rejoice in the Lord, My soul shall be joyful in my God; For He has clothed me with the garments of salvation, He has covered me with the robe of righteousness. Isaiah 61:10a. NKJV

But all these things that I once thought very worthwhile— now I've thrown them all away so that I can put my trust and hope in Christ alone. [8] Yes, everything else is worthless when compared with the priceless gain of knowing Christ Jesus,

My Lord. I have put aside all else, counting it worthless than nothing, in order that I can have Christ. Philippians 3:7-8. The Living Bible, TLB

Don't be weary in prayer; keep at it; watch for God's answers and remember to be thankful when they come. Colossians 4:2, The Living Bible, TLB

As far as the east is from the west, so far has he removed our transgressions from us. Psalm 103:12 NIV

However, I consider my life worth nothing to me, if only I may finish the race and complete the task the Lord Jesus has given me the task of testifying to the gospel of God's grace.

Acts 20:24 NIV

[20] "I do not pray for these alone, but also for those who [a]will believe in Me through their word; [21] that they all may be one, as You, Father, are in Me, and I in You; that they also may be one in Us, that the world may believe that You sent Me. [22] And the glory which You gave Me I have given them, that they may be one just as We are one: [23] I in them, and You in Me; that they may be made perfect in one, and that the world may know that You have sent Me, and have loved them as You have loved Me.

[24] "Father, I desire that they also whom You gave Me may be with Me where I am, that they may behold My glory which You have given Me; for You loved Me before the foundation of the world. 25 O righteous Father! The world has not known You, but I have known You; and these have known that You sent Me. 26 And I have declared to them Your name, and will declare it, that the love with which You loved Me may be in them, and I in them." John 17:24-26 NKJV

WHEN YOU'RE FEELING DOWN DON'T LOOK AROUND, INSTEAD LOOK UP TO THE **ONE** *who* IS ABLE TO KEEP **YOU.** PSALMS 121

A Darlene Gonzales LifeScript

Psalm 121 King James Version (KJV)

[1] I will lift up my eyes unto the hills, from whence cometh my help.

[2] My help cometh from the LORD, which made heaven and earth.

[3] He will not suffer thy foot to be moved: he that keepeth thee will not slumber.

[4] Behold, he that keepeth Israel shall neither slumber nor sleep.

[5] The LORD is thy keeper: the LORD is thy shade upon thy right hand.

[6] The sun shall not smite thee by day, nor the moon by night.

[7] The LORD shall preserve thee from all evil: he shall preserve thy soul.

[8] The LORD shall preserve thy going out and thy coming in from this time forth, and even for evermore.

MY LifeScript **JOURNAL**

AND THEN I WILL NEED GOD'S HELP WITH

MY LifeScript **JOURNAL**

AND THEN I WILL NEED GOD'S HELP WITH

MY LifeScript **JOURNAL**

_____

_____

_____

_____

_____

_____

_____

_____

_____

_____

_____

AND THEN I WILL NEED GOD'S HELP WITH

_____

_____

_____

_____

_____

John 8:36 New King James Version (NKJV)

Therefore, if the Son makes you free,
you shall be free indeed.

MY LifeScript **JOURNAL**

AND THEN I WILL NEED GOD'S HELP WITH

MY LifeScript **JOURNAL**

AND THEN I WILL NEED GOD'S HELP WITH

MY LifeScript **JOURNAL**

AND THEN I WILL NEED GOD'S HELP WITH

do not lose heart

Jude 24-25 King James Version (KJV)
24 Now unto him that is able to keep you from falling, and to present you faultless before the presence of his glory with exceeding joy,
25 To the only wise God our Savior, be glory and majesty, dominion and power, both now and ever. Amen.

A Darlene Gonzales LifeScript

MY LifeScript **JOURNAL**

_____

_____

_____

_____

_____

_____

_____

_____

_____

_____

AND THEN I WILL NEED GOD'S HELP WITH

_____

_____

_____

_____

_____

MY LifeScript **JOURNAL**

_____

_____

_____

_____

_____

_____

_____

_____

_____

_____

AND THEN I WILL NEED GOD'S HELP WITH

_____

_____

_____

_____

_____

MY LifeScript **JOURNAL**

_____

_____

_____

_____

_____

_____

_____

_____

_____

_____

_____

_____

AND THEN I WILL NEED GOD'S HELP WITH

_____

_____

_____

_____

_____

A Darlene Gonzales LifeScript

BEAUTY IS ON THE INSIDE.
HE HAS MADE YOU AND FASHIONED YOU. PSALM 139:14

Psalm 139:14 New King James Version (NKJV)

I will praise You, for I am fearfully *and* wonderfully made;
Marvelous are Your works,
And *that* my soul knows very well.

MY LifeScript **JOURNAL**

AND THEN I WILL NEED GOD'S HELP WITH

MY LifeScript **JOURNAL**

_____

_____

_____

_____

_____

_____

_____

_____

_____

_____

_____

AND THEN I WILL NEED GOD'S HELP WITH

_____

_____

_____

_____

_____

MY LifeScript **JOURNAL**

_____

_____

_____

_____

_____

_____

_____

_____

_____

_____

_____

_____

AND THEN I WILL NEED GOD'S HELP WITH

_____

_____

_____

_____

_____

Don't Argue With A Lie....

Casting down imaginations, and every high thing that exalteth itself against the knowledge of God, and bring into captivity every thought to the obedience of Christ.
2 Corinthians 10:5

MY LifeScript **JOURNAL**

_____

_____

_____

_____

_____

_____

_____

_____

_____

_____

AND THEN I WILL NEED GOD'S HELP WITH

_____

_____

_____

_____

MY LifeScript JOURNAL

AND THEN I WILL NEED GOD'S HELP WITH

MY LifeScript **JOURNAL**

_____

_____

_____

_____

_____

_____

_____

_____

_____

_____

_____

AND THEN I WILL NEED GOD'S HELP WITH

_____

_____

_____

_____

_____

MAKE SURE YOU'RE DRESSED PROPERLY AS YOU LEAVE FOR THE DAY. EPHESIANS 6:10-18

A Darlene Gonzales LifeScript

Ephesians 6:10-18 King James Version (KJV)

[10] Finally, my brethren, be strong in the Lord, and in the power of his might.

[11] Put on the whole armour of God, that ye may be able to stand against the wiles of the devil.

[12] For we wrestle not against flesh and blood, but against principalities, against powers, against the rulers of the darkness of this world, against spiritual wickedness in high places.

[13] Wherefore take unto you the whole armour of God, that ye may be able to withstand in the evil day, and having done all, to stand.

[14] Stand therefore, having your loins girt about with truth, and having on the breastplate of righteousness;

[15] And your feet shod with the preparation of the gospel of peace;

[16] Above all, taking the shield of faith, wherewith ye shall be able to quench all the fiery darts of the wicked.

[17] And take the helmet of salvation, and the sword of the Spirit, which is the word of God: [18] Praying always with all prayer and supplication in the Spirit, and watching thereunto with all perseverance and supplication for all saints;

MY LifeScript **JOURNAL**

AND THEN I WILL NEED GOD'S HELP WITH

MY LifeScript **JOURNAL**

AND THEN I WILL NEED GOD'S HELP WITH

MY LifeScript **JOURNAL**

_____

_____

_____

_____

_____

_____

_____

_____

_____

_____

AND THEN I WILL NEED GOD'S HELP WITH

_____

_____

_____

_____

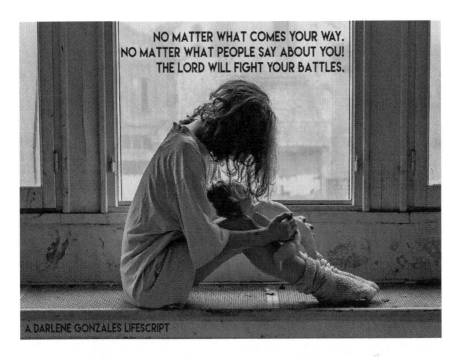

A DARLENE GONZALES LIFESCRIPT

Psalm 119:165 New International Version (NIV)

Great peace have those who love your law,
and nothing can make them stumble.

MY LifeScript **JOURNAL**

_____

_____

_____

_____

_____

_____

_____

_____

_____

_____

_____

_____

AND THEN I WILL NEED GOD'S HELP WITH

_____

_____

_____

_____

_____

MY LifeScript **JOURNAL**

_____

_____

_____

_____

_____

_____

_____

_____

_____

_____

_____

AND THEN I WILL NEED GOD'S HELP WITH

_____

_____

_____

_____

_____

MY LifeScript **JOURNAL**

AND THEN I WILL NEED GOD'S HELP WITH

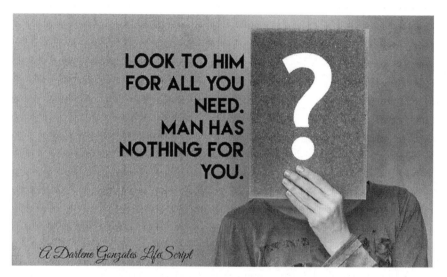

Philippians 4:19 NIV Version

And my God will meet all your needs
according to the riches of His glory by Christ Jesus.

MY LifeScript **JOURNAL**

AND THEN I WILL NEED GOD'S HELP WITH

MY LifeScript **JOURNAL**

_____

_____

_____

_____

_____

_____

_____

_____

_____

_____

_____

AND THEN I WILL NEED GOD'S HELP WITH

_____

_____

_____

_____

_____

MY LifeScript **JOURNAL**

AND THEN I WILL NEED GOD'S HELP WITH

TRUST AND BELIEVE

HE IS EVERYTHING, IF YOU LET HIM, AND IS TAKING CARE OF YOU NOW AND FOREVERMORE.

A Darlene Gonzales LifeScript

Psalm 23 King James Version (KJV)

The LORD is my shepherd; I shall not want.
² He maketh me to lie down in green pastures:
he leadeth me beside the still waters.
³ He restoreth my soul:
he leadeth me in the paths of righteousness for his name's sake.
⁴ Yea, though I walk through the valley of the shadow of death,
I will fear no evil: for thou art with me;
thy rod and thy staff they comfort me.
⁵ Thou preparest a table before me in the presence of mine enemies:
thou anointest my head with oil; my cup runneth over.
⁶ Surely goodness and mercy shall follow me all the days of my life:
and I will dwell in the house of the LORD forever.

MY LifeScript **JOURNAL**

_____

_____

_____

_____

_____

_____

_____

_____

_____

_____

_____

AND THEN I WILL NEED GOD'S HELP WITH

_____

_____

_____

_____

_____

MY LifeScript **JOURNAL**

_____

_____

_____

_____

_____

_____

_____

_____

_____

_____

_____

AND THEN I WILL NEED GOD'S HELP WITH

_____

_____

_____

_____

MY LifeScript **JOURNAL**

AND THEN I WILL NEED GOD'S HELP WITH

MY LifeScript **JOURNAL**

AND THEN I WILL NEED GOD'S HELP WITH

MY LifeScript JOURNAL

_____

_____

_____

_____

_____

_____

_____

_____

_____

_____

AND THEN I WILL NEED GOD'S HELP WITH

_____

_____

_____

_____

_____

MY LifeScript **JOURNAL**

_____

_____

_____

_____

_____

_____

_____

_____

_____

_____

_____

AND THEN I WILL NEED GOD'S HELP WITH

_____

_____

_____

_____

_____

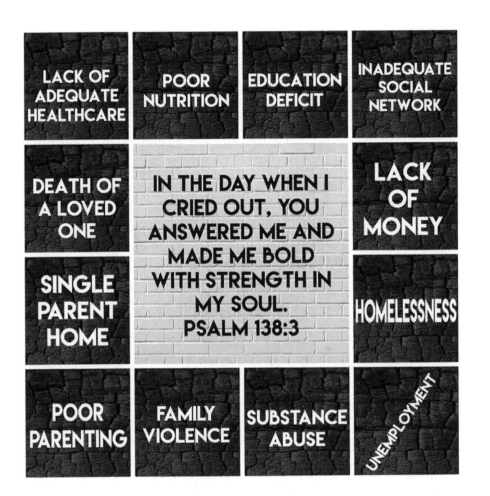

LACK OF
ADEQUATE
HEALTHCARE

POOR
NUTRITION

EDUCATION
DEFICIT

INADEQUATE
SOCIAL
NETWORK

DEATH OF
A LOVED
ONE

IN THE DAY WHEN I
CRIED OUT, YOU
ANSWERED ME AND
MADE ME BOLD
WITH STRENGTH IN
MY SOUL.
PSALM 138:3

LACK
OF
MONEY

SINGLE
PARENT
HOME

HOMELESSNESS

POOR
PARENTING

FAMILY
VIOLENCE

SUBSTANCE
ABUSE

UNEMPLOYMENT

WINDOWS OF TRAUMA

MY LifeScript **JOURNAL**

_____

_____

_____

_____

_____

_____

_____

_____

_____

_____

_____

AND THEN I WILL NEED GOD'S HELP WITH

_____

_____

_____

_____

_____

MY LifeScript **JOURNAL**

_____

_____

_____

_____

_____

_____

_____

_____

_____

_____

AND THEN I WILL NEED GOD'S HELP WITH

_____

_____

_____

_____

_____

MY LifeScript **JOURNAL**

AND THEN I WILL NEED GOD'S HELP WITH

MY LifeScript **JOURNAL**

AND THEN I WILL NEED GOD'S HELP WITH

MY LifeScript **JOURNAL**

AND THEN I WILL NEED GOD'S HELP WITH

MY LifeScript **JOURNAL**

AND THEN I WILL NEED GOD'S HELP WITH

MY LifeScript **JOURNAL**

_____

_____

_____

_____

_____

_____

_____

_____

_____

_____

AND THEN I WILL NEED GOD'S HELP WITH

_____

_____

_____

_____

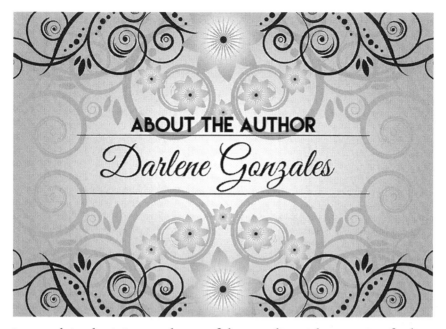

ABOUT THE AUTHOR

Darlene Gonzales

is an ordained minister and powerful evangelist with a growing feeding ministry to the indigent. She is also a trained medical professional, a peer supporter in the mental health field, and a survivor of domestic violence. Her Sunrise is likening unto the 10 lepers in Scripture who were healed as they went. Darlene was delivered by the Power of the Holy Ghost from her addictions. Her passions are for those who have fallen and given up because of the many times they have tried and failed. (Mark 4:14-20). She encourages you by the transparency of her LifeScript and her raw story that if you "Never Give Up, Christ is ready to raise you up!" DARLENE experienced homelessness and chronic addictions, but God delivered her in 2008 from each, and is honored to speak locally and nationally to those who will hear and believe in the saving power of God's Son, Jesus, the Christ. Darlene lives in Tucson, Arizona and is currently considering becoming a Chaplain and acquiring her MSW degree.

For speaking engagements, and individual and group encouragement, Contact Darlene by email at: darlenegonzales48@yahoo.com.

Made in the USA
Columbia, SC
05 December 2022

72348013R00093